Gareth Cliff on Everything

Gareth Cliff on Everything

Gareth Cliff

Jonathan Ball Publishers
Johannesburg & Cape Town

First published in trade paperback in 2011 by
JONATHAN BALL PUBLISHERS (PTY) LTD
PO Box 33977
Jeppestown
2043

ISBN 978 1 86842 455 9

Cover design by Michiel Botha, Cape Town
Cover cartoons by Dean Jensen
Design and layout of text by Triple M Design, Johannesburg
Printed and bound by CTP Book Printers, Cape

Contents

Acknowledgements

This book would never have happened if the publishers hadn't approached me to do it. It is Jeremy Boraine, editor Alfred LeMaitre, Eugene Ashton and the team at Jonathan Ball publishers who deserve the greater part of my thanks. Along with my manager, Rina Broomberg, who cracked the whip and helped me throw out huge chunks of self-indulgent verbosity, we had an idea that a book might work. Naturally I wish to thank my terrific family for at least some of the content: my father and mother, Rory and Monica; and my brother and sister Robert and Sandra. They are the nicest people I know, and sometimes the oddest. Overwhelmingly I must thank the people who listen to my radio show, follow me on Twitter and Facebook, sit through the roller coaster ride of *Idols* and read the articles I have been hammering out on garethcliff.com for the last few years. No doubt they will find themselves familiar with much of the style in this book.

There are many names that I could rattle off as having been valuable to me in the formulation of ideas, giving a context to experiences and influencing my own writing. I won't bore you. Suffice it to say that Mr Liddle from Laddsworth Primary School, John Cleese, Stephen Fry and Christopher Hitchens have probably had more to do with my love of words than any other people, and I credit them with an umbrella acknowledgement for any part of this book which they may have influenced – consciously or not. I hope I won't upset or offend you. Plato said: 'Wise men talk because they have something to say; fools, because they have to say something.' I hope you will not judge me of the latter category.

Opinions are like arseholes – everybody has one

Wow, you're very opinionated!', she said in a disgusted tone, walking away in a hurry in case I gave her one more. I don't know why, but some people think it a very bad thing to have an opinion about anything. Blend in, don't make too much noise, just be happy with what you know and do. That seems to be their motto. I couldn't do that. The woman in question was a conservative, middle-aged mother of two who probably worked for a bank, was out of love with her husband, watched a lot of TV soap operas and drove, at best, a Volvo. People like that consider people with opinions dangerous for the common good. But that's just my opinion.

From the bold to the beautiful: I met a really pretty girl in 2004. She was sexy, vivacious, educated and talented, and even had a great sense of humour. Everything seemed to be just about perfect. The only problem was that she had no opinion on anything. She didn't think abortion was right, or wrong. She didn't know or care whether there was global warming. She didn't want to talk politics, religion, race, culture or news (you know, all the good stuff). In a situation like this, you can't really have a good conversation; she never said what she thought or how she felt. She could only really talk about herself or laugh at me. It was a pity because I might have fathered some offspring with her. Did I mention that she really was very pretty?

I suppose you might think me petty for making a big deal about something like opinions, but it's actually a really big reason that I will either get on with you or not. Imagine how difficult it would be to have friends of a different race and another friend who's a racist. Things would get complicated because the racist holds an unacceptable opinion. You see, it *is* a big deal.

If you really believe it's important to be free (and I assume you do, since the alternative is slavery or serfdom), then you have to exercise your freedom. What would be the point of having a guitar if you never learnt to play it? Freedom needs to be put to work – you need to keep it fit. The best way to exercise your freedom is to decide how you feel about the things you care about, and let other people know. If you think the government is screwing things up, you need to tell them. If you think being overcharged for bread is wrong, and you never say anything, the people who make and sell the bread will keep taking advantage of you, and ripping you off. Wait a second, that actually did happen …

Throughout human history, people have been subjects, forced to fit in with someone else's opinion of how things should work – a king, emperor, Pope or Führer. Thanks to the arduous struggle of the Enlightenment, the abolition of slavery, the spread of democracy, universal suffrage, the destruction of racism and increased access to education and information, we are only now able to voice our own opinions. We should guard this right jealously, just in case the politicians decide to chip away at it again. Authority doesn't like opinion; it likes obedience. Don't think for a minute that those in power enjoy our being able to argue with them. The only reason we have rubbish governments is because so many ordinary people have no opinions.

So what opinions do you have? What matters to you? If I asked you how you feel about what children should be taught at school, what you think about corruption, who you think would be freakier in bed – Lady Gaga or Courtney Love – you'd surely have an answer?

You see what I mean by this? Being opinionated is not about grandstanding and shoving your thoughts down other people's throats; it's the whole point of being free. If you have no opinions about anything, you can't be a very thoughtful or serious person (and by this I mean a person to be taken seriously, rather than someone who is always solemn). What you think about tells the world more about you than how you look or what you have. How interested you are in the world will determine how interested the world is in you. That's why opinion matters – because you matter. If you don't think you matter, don't worry, you don't need opinions – I've already made up my mind about you.

This has to go

There are things I have seen around in the last while that are pointless, that serve no purpose at all and that need to be thrown out along with the old loom, wooden tennis racket and patchwork leather jacket. Tell me if you agree.

1 The paperwork you have to complete upon entering an office park, complex or golf estate

I don't understand this procedure at all. It was thought up by terrified white people, and they think it works. As a matter of principle, I fill in 'Mickey Mouse' under *name*, 'Disneyworld' under *address* and 555-5555 under *contact number*. If they have a column for *Reason for entry* I just say 'To have sex'. Nobody seems ever to have noticed. Just let me in. What kind of burglar, rapist or murderer is going to leave their correct details at the gate?

2 Nigella Lawson

Look, sweetheart, we know you married the world's richest ad man and you like to eat (sometimes your arse is all we can fit on the screen), but it's time you stopped messing around and just went straight into porn. Everything is 'succulent, juicy, dripping, sensual, exotic, erotic and moist' – and we know you're not talking about food. Get on with it; stop trying to make middle-aged recipe shows sexy. Just take it off or be gone.

3 Those 'Power Plate' things at the gym

It's only ever obese people on them. I don't know what they do. They shake you around or something. You won't get thin being shaken around only, so stop wasting your time. Eat less, run more. That's my diet. It will work; Power Plate will not.

4 Scanners for your bags

I once walked into the SABC carrying a sharp, cold-steel cavalry sabre. It's a big shiny sword, as long as your leg. They asked me to put it through the scanner. Every morning I have to remove my laptop from my bag and put it through the scanner at work, and every week I do the same at the airport. Someone decided this was important, and now we're forced to waste time doing it. Not one of those Einsteins behind the screen would be able to identify illicit or explosive material anyway, so why do we bother? Al-Qaeda could have smuggled an entire Boeing 747 in pieces through OR Tambo and the 'scoo-rty' wouldn't have batted an eyelid.

5 The Opening of Parliament

It's not fashionable or exciting, or classy or smart, or even interesting. The President READS out a dreary speech in a monotone; loads of overweight, dishevelled-looking women wear bright clothes covering up their less-than-sexy bodies and the opposition always says that 'It was alright, but ...' We endure the sight of Leanne Manas and Vuyo Mbuli falling over themselves to line up ministers for interviews, and the presidential guard can't march in time with each other or the music. Dispense with the ceremony; it looks like a primary school concert. Just get to work, politicians, nobody cares about your self-aggrandisement.

6 The word 'community'

Everything seems to be about the community. Nothing is about individuals any more. This is the root of many of our problems, from lack of personal responsibility to corruption, deceit and the aggregation of power in dark corners. A community must be very clearly defined in order to be considered anything less than nebulous. Most people who use the word use it as a euphemism, and may as well use the word 'herd', 'troop' or 'coven' in its place. It would have the same effect, but gain much in descriptive value.

7 *Twilight* movies

We can all see through Stephenie Meyer's plagiarised amalgamation of *Romeo and Juliet*, *Nosferatu* and *The Glass Menagerie*. It's tired. Sure, a bunch of awkward, gawky, screechy teenage girls think they're Bella and love the books and the movies, but we should all be embarrassed by the way Meyer keeps churning them out, like a second-rate JK Rowling. It's about SEX, girls, and in the real world both Edward Cullen and the werewolf guy would have had sex with her and/or moved on by now. You need to do the same ...

Every day some weird new and unnecessary task, device, item or thought will make itself evident. Some of these don't need to be taken seriously; like Al Gore, they'll eventually go away if we ignore them ...

Dear Government

27 October 2010

Dear Government,

OK, I get it; the President isn't the only one in charge. The ANC believes in 'collective responsibility' (so that nobody has to get blamed when things get screwed up), so I address this to everyone in government – the whole lot of you – good, bad and ugly (that's you, Blade).

We were all so pleased with your renewed promises to deliver services (we'll forgive the fact that in some places people are worse off than in 1994), to root out corruption (so far, your record is worse than under Mbeki, Mandela or the apartheid regime, what with family members becoming overnight millionaires) and build infrastructure (state tenders going disgustingly awry and pretty stadia standing empty notwithstanding), and with the good job you did when FIFA were telling you what to do for a few months this year. Give yourselves half a pat on the back. Since President Sepp went off with his billions, I'm afraid we have less to be proud of – public service strikes, more presidential bastard children, increasing unemployment and a lack of leadership that allowed the unions to make the elected government its bitch. You should be more than a little worried – but you're not. Hence my letter. Here are some things that might have passed you by:

1 You have to stop corruption

Don't stop it because rich people moan about it and because it makes poor people feel that you are self-enriching parasites of state resources, but because it is a disease that will kill us all. It's simple: there is only so much money left to be plundered. When that money runs out, the plunderers will raise taxes, chase and drain all the remaining cash out of the country and be left with nothing but the rotting remains of what could have been the greatest success story of post-colonial Africa. It's called corruption because it decomposes the fabric of society. When someone is found guilty of corruption, don't go near them – it's catching. Making yourself rich at the country's expense is what colonialists do.

2 Stop complaining about the media

You're only complaining about them because they show you up for how little you really do or care. If you were trying really hard, and you didn't drive the most expensive car in the land, or have a nephew who suddenly went from modest obscurity to ostentatious opulence, we'd have only positive things to report. Think of Jay Naidoo, Geraldine Fraser-Moleketi and Zwelinzima Vavi: they come under a lot of fire, but it's never embarrassing. It's always about their ideas, their positions, and is perfectly acceptable criticism for people in power to put up with. When the media go after Blade Nzimande, Siphiwe Nyanda and the President, they say we need a new piece of legislation to 'make the media responsible'. That's because they're being humiliated by the facts we uncover about them daily, not because there is an agenda in some newsroom. If there had been a free press during the reigns of Henry VIII, Idi Amin or Hitler, their regimes might just have been kept a little less destructive, and certainly would have been less brazen and unchecked.

3 Education is a disaster

We're the least literate and numerate country in Africa. Zimbabwe produces better school results and turns out smarter kids than we do. Our youth aren't unemployed; they're unemployable. Outcomes-based education, teachers' unions and an attitude of mediocrity that discourages excellence have reduced us to a laughing stock. Our learners can't spell, read, add or subtract. What are all these people going to do? Become President? There's only one job like that. We need clever people, not average or stupid ones. The failure of the education department happened on your watch. Someone who writes matric now hadn't even started school under the apartheid regime, so you cannot blame anyone but yourselves for this colossal cock-up. Fix it before three quarters of our matrics end up begging on Oxford Road. Reward schools and teachers who deliver great pass rates and clever students into the system. Fire the teachers who march and neglect their classrooms.

4 Give up on BEE

It isn't working. Free shares for new black partnerships in old white companies has made everyone poorer except for Tokyo Sexwale. Giving people control of existing business won't make more jobs either. In fact, big companies aren't growing; they're reducing staff and costs. The key is entrepreneurship. People with initiative, creative ideas and small companies must be given tax breaks and assistance. Young black professionals must be encouraged to start their own businesses rather than join the board of a big corporation as their token black shareholder or director. Government must also stop thinking that state employment is a way to decrease unemployment; it isn't – it's a tax burden. India and China are churning out brilliant, qualified people at a rate that makes us look like losers. South Africa has a proud history of innovation, pioneering and genius. This is the only way we can advance our society and economy beyond merely coping.

5 Stop squabbling over power

Offices are not there for you to occupy (or be deployed to) and aggrandise yourself. Offices in government are there to provide a service. If you think outrageous salaries, big German cars, first-class travel and state housing are the reasons to aspire to leadership, you're in the wrong business – you should be working for a dysfunctional, tumbledown parastatal (or Glenn Agliotti). We don't care who the Chairperson of the National Council of Provinces is if we don't have running water, electricity, schools and clean streets. You work for us. Do your job; don't imagine you *are* your job.

6 Stop renaming things

Build new things to name. If I live in a street down which the sewage runs, I don't care if it's called Hans Strijdom or Malibongwe. Calling it something nice and new won't make it smell nice and new. Rebranding is something Cell C does with Trevor Noah, not something you can whitewash your lack of delivery with.

7 Don't think you'll be in power forever

People aren't as stupid as you think we are. We know you sit around laughing about how much you get away with. We'll take you down, either at the polls or – if it comes down to the wire – by revolution (yes, Julius, the real kind, not the one you imagine happened in 2008). Careless, wasteful and wanton government is a thing of the past. The days of thin propaganda and idealised struggle are over. The people put you in power – they will take you out of it. Africa is tired of tinpot dictators, one-party states and banana republics. We know who we are now, we care about our future – and so should you.

Dear Government II: the aftermath

28 October 2010

I am a little surprised by the reaction to my 'Dear Government' letter. Many have said they support the sentiment, a few have decried it as rubbish, and some have made the point that while they agree with the content, they cannot condone the tone. I thank you for any replies you may have sent me or have thought of sending me.

To address the emotive issue of the tone of the letter, I must offer some explanation. If I sound overly aggressive, then it is due to a build-up of frustration with the concerns I raised in the letter. For this I cannot apologise without being dishonest. What I will apologise for, if asked, is any perceived personal insult. It was certainly not my intention to pick a fight or to slight individuals. This apology having been offered, the issues remain and must be addressed. I might add that I am a proud descendant of many bastards, and that I don't consider the term abusive, and that 'The Good, the Bad, and the Ugly' is a movie title, a song and a joke. Mr Nzimande may interpret this as a slur on his good looks if he so wishes – I was referring to his attitude.

Might I add that I don't believe the President is as touchy or thin-skinned as all his erstwhile defenders seem to intimate he is? Our President has been insulted far more brutally and more directly by the National Prosecuting Authority, any number of cartoonists and a rabble of journalists, protestors, opposition politicians and trade union leaders over the years. Having been in very real peril so often during the struggle and after – in his own personal struggles – I'm quite sure the President does not think my insult the worst.

That done, I have had almost no replies whatsoever from anyone who takes issue with the content of the letter and offers a sensible counter-argument. This leads me to believe that the reason my letter is being widely circulated and supported is because it contains obvious home truths and not because it is any kind of revealed wisdom. A few 'love me too, daddy' responses have been issued by Professor Jansen, Jeremy Gordin and Nigel Pierce, but I confess I have seen nothing novel in any of their contributions. It is clear they are grumpy about the bandwagon leaving before they could hop on it, and they all evidence their perfectly acceptable dislike of me. Go to it, gentlemen: work a little harder.

What is impressive about this exercise is the increase in the scale of the public debate thanks to the internet. Immediate, insightful, evolving threads of discussion have unwound from the dissemination of the original letter, and this is very encouraging. I am pleased to see that so many South Africans care so passionately about our country, regardless of whether we agree or disagree. The old 'letters to the editor' means of airing issues of importance has been replaced by an organic, direct and instant forum for conversation. Surely this is something we can be very proud of? Newspapers, radio stations and television seem to lag behind ever more as we all become broadcasters online. Let it never again be said that young people in South Africa are apathetic, disengaged and ill-informed. There are new ways of finding facts, starting arguments and getting to the things that matter. The fourth estate is no longer the province of a few editors and spin doctors.

I was amused to have a serious journalist ask me if I thought the Office of the President might ban me from writing again. I thought this betrayed his own opinion of government and the free media more than any answer I could give. All week I have had journalists stoking fires, manufacturing tensions and making it look like I was engaged in a battle to the death with government. Questions like 'Have you been threatened by powerful politicians?', 'Are you scared that the Presidency will go after you?' and even 'Do you stand by what you wrote?' (What kind of people do they usually ask that of, and what other answer could there be but 'yes'?)

Instead the calm voice of reason has been the Office of the President. They requested a meeting to discuss matters raised in the letter – simple, honest, reasonable and, I hope, positive. We live in a country that knows freedom better than most, because we come from a history that knew none. Let us celebrate the right to have opinions, speak truth to power and disagree in a civil manner. Despite everything I raised in my letter, I am prouder and more dedicated to South Africa than I ever have been.

Dear Government III: the journey continues ...

10 November 2010

People love bitching, don't they? At work, at dinner, at parties, even in bed with their husband or wife. Bitching about government is something we're very good at. It takes up a lot of our time and nothing really comes of it, other than all of us getting it off our chests. Most of us feel like we can't really make a difference, so we never do anything to get our hands dirty, and most of the time we're right. A week or two ago, I decided to tell government what worried me about South Africa, instead of keeping it to myself. I think it was a good idea.

In the last two weeks, in response to the 'Dear Government' letter I posted on my website, I've been inundated with messages, calls, e-mails, postings and SMSs from South Africans of all shapes and sizes, old and young, black and white, rich and poor. All these people said more or less the same thing: 'You said exactly what I was thinking!' This doesn't mean I'm a genius of any kind, it just means we all know what's wrong with South Africa and I said it. It was clear that many of us shared the same concerns, values, fears and hopes. For the first time in a long time, we could all find some common ground – we cared.

I heard writer Mark Gevisser saying that we're a manic-depressive country – prone to incredible highs like the World Cup and 1994, and miserable, inconsolable lows like the public servants' strike of September. Maybe we need to calm down and remember that, as a young nation, we have a rocky road to travel – and that we're no more or less special than any other country. Or are we?

We have a lot of diversity to cope with; this is probably something you're tired of hearing, but it's a unique gift. In an increasingly globalised world, people who cope best with diversity are likely to be the ones who benefit most from what the world has to offer. People who isolate themselves will be left behind. So, that said, are we dealing with our diversity positively? I don't think we are.

Let's talk about *Idols*. Every year brings a new race row, a new controversy over the judges, the votes, the winner. This year was no exception. I made a comment about eight weeks back about how I thought it was time for a black Idol and that the blacks in the show were doing a better job than the whites. It was an observation – like saying the girls are better than the boys, and that a girl should win. I'm a judge on the show and that's what I did – I evaluated the talent and made a finding. For some reason, I found myself being called a racist by white people. Most of them asked me why I even brought race up, and why was it necessary to comment on a black or white contestant, as if they were somehow capable of seeing everyone in shades of grey. I was shocked. Some of these people even vowed to vote along racial lines just to prove me wrong (which to them didn't seem racist at all). Most of them, so deeply and patently obsessed with the race of the contestants themselves, expected me to be dishonest enough to pretend that race was not one of the single biggest factors in any sphere of South African society. I'm afraid I couldn't do that.

These same people insisted that they saw race as a non issue, but proceeded to write the most vicious, scathing and derogatory things on various social media platforms that evidenced their inability to see talent in all its multicultural, diverse glory. To them, everything would have been fine if I hadn't brought it up. Fine for them, because their heads could continue to be buried in the sand. I brought it up and they were forced to confront some uncomfortable truths about their own way of thinking.

It hardly mattered that a few weeks later I was being called a racist by some blacks, this time over my critical letter to government. Do you suppose the two badges cancel each other out?

We complain about government, we insist that they must bring about positive change, but we ourselves seldom leave our comfort zones. We think we've achieved a great deal when we go and watch rugby in a township stadium, or when we have a few white friends at our *shisa nyama*. These things are so superficial. We're making the minimum of effort, and even there it's just to tolerate each other.

I'm not suggesting social engineering or forced socialisation, but I do insist that we get our attitudes right. You don't need to suddenly find yourself an Indian boyfriend, learn the words to 'Izinja' by Mapaputsi, or move to Vryheid to prove you can cope with diversity; just decide you will. Start with a sincere connection: admit that you thought the driver in front of you was Chinese, or a woman, or stupid, until you drove past and saw it was your Dad's friend. Acknowledge your share of the prejudice, and own it so that you don't do it again. I might sound like Dr Phil here, but we all need some therapy. Miracles don't happen; positive change requires hard work.

So I'll write my letters, and continue to challenge government, not because I hate them but because I expect more from them. South Africa belongs to all of us. I am encouraged by their response to my letter – not to gag me but rather to engage with me. They even encouraged me to keep writing and to keep making jokes … but to stop calling people ugly.

No single person should matter more than the next. Next time you're about to start bitching about government (or *Idols*), ask yourself if you did something valuable for the country today. Not something for yourself, for the country. If you did something, you can complain all you like. If you didn't, get off your butt and go and do something. Positive people in Africa are lining themselves up to take advantage of one of the last unsaturated global markets, rich in material resources and potential. If you're not interested in your country, why should your country be interested in you?

Holidays 101

The holidays might be something you've been craving all year. We all love the end-of-year break, and we need it quite badly. There's just one problem: you forgot about all the things that ruined last December for you because it was a whole year ago. Let me explain: there are things about the holidays that can bite you in the backside and turn what should be a festive, relaxing time into a nightmare. Here are ten tips for a happy holiday.

1 You don't need to go away to get away

There's so much pressure to make the December holiday count. Some people splash out and go to Cuba, America, the Seychelles or Bali. Cape Town, Plett, Sodwana and Ballito can be just as relaxing, and won't give you headaches when you do your finances in February. You also might not need three weeks. One week is sometimes enough. Don't be so self-indulgent.

2 Ninety per cent of us don't have beach-fit bodies,

so we're not going to feel too good about being scantily clad in public. You forget how awful you felt when someone you liked last year commented on how hot that other guy on the beach looked, while glaring disapprovingly at you. Just accept that nobody wants to look at you, and make the most of your time on the beach. Which brings me, conveniently, to point three.

3 You're going to eat too much,

feel stuffed and have indigestion from all the rich holiday food. You'll put on a ton of weight, you'll sweat in the heat, and you'll hate your body in January. We all think we can moderate this, but we can't. Christmas, especially, is pig-out time. Leftovers don't help, and neither do the old ladies in every family who feel that their holiday duties consist of them force-feeding you cholesterol-packed rubbish like stuffing and fatty red meat. Just learn to say no. Start practising now.

4 You might meet some people on holiday

Even with the best of intentions, it is unlikely that these cool new people will still be in your life by June. Normally you're already bored with them by the end of the holiday. Maybe they're bored with you, too. You're not going to meet your new best friend on holiday. Be happy with the people you're with – family, friends, a lover – and forget about that cool group of guys you hung out with at the bar, the girls who you met in the swimwear section, or the celebrity who rented the house next to yours and came round to borrow some booze. They're holiday friends.

5 You'll feel guilty that you wish you were single

every day you're away with your boyfriend or girlfriend. On holiday you'll feel a bit hedonistic, you'll be caught up in the joy of the holidays and the sense of reckless abandon, and you'll behave like a single person – but you might not be. This will put your relationship under severe strain because there will be many opportunities for whirlwind romances and fun nights out, but you'll have to stay in and do 'couple things'. You may end up watching a lot of DVDs. Combat this feeling by accepting the benefits of reliable sex, or split up before the holidays start. If you really love the one you're with, this tip is invalid.

6 Don't spend all your money

Buy everyone a small, sentimental gift rather than splashing out on a Pierneef for your mom, just because you're feeling guilty that she sacrificed her best years raising you. If you don't buy something small for that great-aunt you usually ignore, she'll harbour a grudge for many years. The Christmas table will be a miserable place for you when she hands you a crummy gift and you have nothing but a smile and reluctant kiss for the old bitch.

7 Your presents will be OK

You're not seven years old anymore. When you're seven, all those presents under the tree stir up an intense excitement that is the closest any human being comes to experiencing real magic. On the night you expect Father Christmas, every sound is a clue to his being there. You're so excited that your little heart beats like an older person suffering from severe cardiac arrhythmia. When you open that present the next day, it is the best thing that ever happened to you. That doesn't happen after you turn 23. You know it'll be something practical, domestic or partially edible. Shopping for yourself is more fun. Actually, do that instead.

8 New Year's Eve is going to be disappointing

I know I shouldn't be so pessimistic, but there's so much hype around NYE that people expect it to outclass every other party they've ever had. Chances are that it won't live up to your very high expectations. You won't even remember the countdown, and there will be annoying people pushing and jostling to kiss you and whoever you're with, so you might even end up in a drunken brawl. You'll drink too much yourself, lose your phone or wake up with a throbbing headache and a hundred text messages from people whose numbers you deleted two years ago. Just go with the flow and stay more sober than the person on your left … Unless Charlie Sheen is the person on your left.

9 You might miss work

Not pine after the actual labour, but the routine, the office jokes, the sense of purpose. About halfway into your holiday you may start feeling guilty about things you didn't do in the past year, and you might get a little excited about what you could still do in the coming year. This too will pass, but you'll notice it becoming more apparent when you hear screaming kids, get badly sunburnt or wake up very hung-over. Forget about it. Work still sucks.

10 You're going to be poor in January

You'll forget all about your fabulous holiday, your tan will fade, you'll be tired within the first week, and people will ask you where you went and what you did for the first three hours of your first day back. After that, they won't care, so don't keep telling them about the parasailing or the episode with the crocodile in the lagoon or when your wife slipped in the waves and her enormous breasts popped out of her top. Some of them worked through the holidays and they hate you. Just smile.

So whatever happens, whoever plots to screw up your time off, and no matter how bad the bad times are, holidays tend to be windows for some great memories to be made. You deserve them.

Giving a sacrificial damn

Someone has to say it: ancestor worship and animal sacrifice are not part of your culture, inseparable from your identity. They're outdated, primitive, unnecessary rituals which make you an easy target for racists who think you haven't caught up to the 21st century.

Before we even get into this messy business of throat-cutting and complaining to the dead, let me go on record and say that I think all religion is nonsense and I don't believe in the supernatural at all. In fact, I struggle to take you seriously if you say you do. In other words, what I am about to say with respect to our own country's backward beliefs applies just as much to the three great monotheisms (Judaism, Christianity and Islam) and all the wacky religious philosophies of the East. *Ergo*, you cannot claim to be my exclusive victim. At least here I am an equal-opportunity offender.

Once upon a time, in the dank recesses of caves and on the windy tops of sacred mountains, Bronze-age humans used to perform violent and cruel propitiations to keep their gods happy. They did it for Zeus, Jupiter, Ra and Woden, among others. They did it with knives and stones and fire. They did it to goats, sheep, cattle and even humans … even children! The religious rites of the Aztecs are reckoned to have put an end to some 20 000 or more innocent human lives, with the high priest ripping the still-beating heart from the chest cavity of the victim.

The foundation story of Abrahamic monotheism has it that Abraham was quite ready to sacrifice his own son to show his faith – and was indeed deemed praiseworthy for this immoral and disgusting readiness. It is telling that this wickedness started an attitude to human sacrificial murder, which extended well into the first century AD, whereby Christians believe God himself succeeded in doing what Abraham had been spared, that is, having his own son murdered. I don't know how the religious teachers navigate this moral minefield, but I will choose to opt out of their babbling and incoherent nonsense about scapegoating just so that I can stick to what I said we'd discuss. Not to put too fine a point on it, by 2011 we consider this kind of behaviour barbaric, and we would see justice done in a court of law to any man who tried to murder his own son, or another person, because he heard voices in his head. It is no longer acceptable to kill people in the name of any gods. Not one of them. If you do, you will be locked up in jail or in a mental asylum.

In Africa, there are long-standing traditions and customs with regard to animal sacrifice, and a committed link between the living and the dead, most often displayed in various forms of ancestor worship and prayer. You are free to believe anything you like, just as I am free to tell you that I don't and that I think it silly. Tradition and culture have lately tried to place themselves behind the same monolithic, once-impenetrable concrete wall as religion. Who hasn't heard about Jacob Zuma claiming all kinds of cultural vindication for his sexual advances toward women who are not his wives? Who has not seen fundamentalists claiming that it is worse to offend against culture than to speak plainly about things that are retrogressive and contrary to the advance of civilisation? That wall is falling down for religion, so culture and tradition haven't even got a chance. Admit that you just like the feeling of belonging to something, and quietly recite poetry together. That's benign and socially acceptable. Hacking at a bull's throat and bathing in its entrails is not. Don't take my word for it; think about what you look like while you're doing it. You look like a caveman.

I'm not a committed animal rights activist like my sister. She believes animals deserve the same protection from violence and cruelty that we humans do. I couldn't countenance that because I like steak and, frankly, that's what livestock is for. Before humans selectively bred these animals, they didn't roam around in herds like elephant or bison. They didn't exist. They're artificial animals, like toy dogs, and have been adapted for purpose by humans. You see, I'm not romantic about them. I do think that causing malicious harm to any living creature is the sign of a sick mind and that people who hurt animals very often end up hurting people, too. It is often told by those who study serial murderers that in childhood these killers also tormented animals.

If, like me, you want steak, abattoirs aren't perfect, but they're better than letting a bull bleed slowly to death in a township back yard. Plus, even if you believe that the ritual does something profitable for you, nothing to this extent has ever been proven and either makes you seem gullible and full of wishful thinking, or just cruel. Which of those is the least insulting? Pick one. It certainly makes the children uneasy. That should be the first sign that it might be wrong.

There are many traditions that my ancestors used to consider essential: murdering and raping the Scots, for example. But these things are not great illustrations of the content of our character in 2011. As Martin Luther King Jr said, that is all we should be judged by. Culture, race, tradition and religion keep separating us, more and more, from our common humanity. While I would think a world without these things might be arid and colourless, they need to be appreciated as quirky relics from our past, not as defining principles for our future.

If you asked me who I take more seriously, the person who is proud of their history and sees it as a road to their present, or the person who sees their past as a route map for their future, I would have to say the former. The sad reality of the insistence on respect for tradition, culture and history is that the people who most insist on it are the ones who know the least about their own history. Most invoke the ancestors but cannot tell you the name of but one of their great-grandparents, or show you a stone their people turned over in the 1800s. This is not tradition; it's a made-up-on-the-spot fable. Since we don't insist on the veracity of Snow White and the Seven Dwarfs, we must say that religion has no better claim to be considered real history than do the adventures of Dopey, Sleepy or Doc. As someone who respects the study of the human story, I consider that at least hints at some self-respect among those who seek to learn about the past.

Finally, I really don't like the idea of human sacrifice; I don't want anyone to be murdered in my name and I won't give up my personal responsibilities to be borne by another. That is properly unethical. I also don't think that an innocent animal, let alone a child, ought ever to be ritually sacrificed to any god or ancestor who shows by their conspicuous absence at the very most apathy towards the idea of sacrifice. But I hate to disappoint my enemies by leaving them without a solution, and so I propose this to those hell-bent on sacrifice: offer yourself up. Stab yourself on top of a high mountain and mumble some holy words as you expire. You'll make the greatest sacrifice possible to your god and simultaneously rid the planet of one more unnecessary crackpot. Do it; it's the best you can do.

Is this the best you can do?

You hear it all the time in the news, right? There's a leadership crisis! That's what the politicians (ironically supposed to *be* the leaders) keep saying. It's a very big problem in the ANC, where the man we call our President is actually the bargain-bin, most-things-to-most-people, least offensive compromise candidate for a few warring factions under the 'broad church' that is the ruling party. How did we come to this place?

The culture of the ANC, as any stalwart will tell you, is a collective one. The credit for liberation is shared; the blame for the nastier things is shared. Nobody rules alone; consensus is required. This is why you'll hear the secretary-general say things like 'The ANC believes …' and that's also why you'll never see ambition treated with anything but scorn by the rest of the party. Stick your head up above the parapet and they'll shoot it off … And so, many truly charismatic, clever men – Cyril Ramaphosa, Jay Naidoo, Tito Mboweni, Thabo Mbeki, Tokyo Sexwale, Matthews Phosa and the like – find themselves less popular than the louder, rabble-rousing, mouth-breathing types in the NWC and NEC.

In the days of Oliver Tambo, Nelson Mandela, Walter and Albertina Sisulu and Chief Albert Luthuli, the greatest men were expected to be greater still than their white counterparts – to drive the injustice of apartheid even more plainly out of the dark corners and into the light. These men were leaders not because they had a mass of support (even though they did), but because they were right. They were upstanding. History was on their side. They could never be brought to heel by factionalism, uneducated demands for the unrealistic, or by petty union officials. The modern ANC culture makes it very difficult for leaders to emerge, unless by compromise or force. While this culture protects individuals from bearing the brunt of public anger and possible sacking (Alec Erwin springs to mind as one who so totally cocked up everything he touched, but remained long in office), it doesn't foster excellence. The ANC doesn't want excellent men or women. For all his faults (and it is a good thing we are rid of him), Thabo Mbeki was the last man of any excellence to hold high office.

People ask why ANC-run municipalities perform so poorly in delivering services to the people who beg for them. It's because the lower-level politicians are lower-level capable – no excellence. People ask why there are no thinkers taking the party message to the next level and steering the national conscience toward the poor and the needy, to growth, development, national unity, exploring what it means to be South African – no excellence. People ask why the Minister of Higher Education has a fragile ego and no ambition to improve the standard and quality of higher education – an insistence on excellence would count him out of the running. It's all rhetoric, populism and name-calling. Just like high school popularity contests. How desperately disappointing. The voters deserve something better; the ANC deserves something better; the country deserves something better.

Imagine that I ask you to select a team to win the World Cup, but I allow you to choose only the players that the rest of the players aren't threatened by, the ones who play to the crowd, and the ones who don't want to score goals in case it makes the others jealous. Add to that the condition that none of them can be fired, regardless of their lack of skill, talent, discipline or motivation, and they must all be paid the same, regardless of how many goals they score. Their loyalty, not ability, is prized above all. They're also not allowed to disagree publicly, even if the fans want to know what they really think. You're not really selecting anything at all, are you? You've got Scunthorpe United rather than Manchester United. This is the problem with the ANC. Occasionally, an amazingly competent, insightful, pragmatic minister delivers and does us all a favour, but instead of being held aloft as a possible future leader, his or her best bet is to blend in and share the credit. It's not sensible; it's not even Darwinian.

These people eventually retire and/or become successful businesspeople, but the ANC loses them. More's the pity.

The delicate balance between a centrist, individualist party structure and a consensus-based, communal collective is hard to maintain, but the pendulum swung first too far toward the former and recently too far to the latter. The ANC must find this balance, encourage the best among its 'broad church' to accept high office and look to nurture talent in those with potential, or it will be overrun with demagogues and apathetic lame ducks. Our future depends on it.

Tiger, Tiger

On the same day that Tiger Woods fell out with his wife and crashed his car, so did Piet Grobler of Postmasburg. The only difference is that Piet Grobler wasn't on Sky News or in the tabloids. Only his upset mother, his wife Grizelda and the eldest of their children know what's going on. Piet and his skelm snuck into the Hotel Formula One on a business trip to Krugersdorp and they've been texting each other since then. She used to work for him in the 1990s, and knew his wife. While he was in the shower one evening, Piet's wife Grizelda heard his Nokia phone beep. She picked it up and read the message: 'Oooh ek mis jo … Ek l inni bad en dink aan daai aand in Kr'dorp ;).' Poor Grizelda felt the blood rush to her head and she climbed into the shower and started hitting Piet. He had no idea what was going on. Piet and Grizelda now sleep in different beds, but keep up appearances for the children's sake.

When Piet Grobler heard about Tiger Woods, he felt much better. Now he's retelling the story, with relish. Piet feels that because Tiger did all that stuff, he's the same as Piet – but he really isn't like Tiger at all. Tiger is a very talented, very rich, superstar arsehole. Piet is just an arsehole.

That's the thing about fame: everyone loves to see famous people doing regular things, and they love even more to see the good and the great fail. 'Oh look – Tiger Woods cheated! I can't believe it!' Pure, unadulterated *schadenfreude*. It's not just Tiger; it's Jacob Zuma, David Letterman, Joost van der Westhuizen, David Beckham, Arnold Schwarzenegger. Take your pick, they've all entertained the proletariat with their philandering.

What happens is that, for a while, the celebrity is embarrassed and dogged by journalists. Then, within months, they're bigger than ever before, selling books, filling stadia and earning major appearance fees. While Tiger will likely go on doing impressive things and making money, poor old Piet will just pay maintenance for the rest of his life – and his wife's mates will hiss at him in the street.

The Loftus faithful

I have to admit right from the start that I am impressed. For the last three years, about 70 000 people have gathered at Loftus in Pretoria. Was it for rugby? Was it for a politician? Was it for a rock concert? Was it for free stuff? None of the above; it was cultural.

The headliner of these events is Angus Buchan, a KwaZulu-Natal potato farmer who evidently doubles as an evangelist. He arrived to rapturous applause, wearing a leather hat and blue shirt, and told his story and other evidently inspiring stories to the throngs of faithful assembled to hear some good news. I'll talk about religion another time. Right now, there is something else that worries me.

The fact that it was an almost entirely white and almost entirely Afrikaans crowd shouldn't surprise any of us. They've had more than their fair share of bad news and guilt since 1994. They needed to feel good about something, I suppose, and I applaud them for gathering for something positive, even if I don't understand any of it. This conglomeration always happens when any group in any place feels marginalised and dispossessed. Since they started chanting 'De La Rey' a few years back, the Afrikaner population haven't had much to culturally or spiritually bind them together or uplift them. This guy Angus, in combination with the ever-popular Jesus, might just do the trick.

Let me put forward my Afrikaner credentials right now in case the whole of that community starts to complain about me as a 'verraaier' or 'rooinek' from the outside looking in. I am descended from three of the four great leaders of Die Groot Trek. My great-grandfather was the founder of the Tweede-Taalbeweging, and my great-grandmother laid the cornerstone of the Voortrekker Monument. Pretoria is named after my four great-grandfathers, and although two of my great-grandparents fought in the

Anglo-Boer War, they were respectively on opposing sides. I attended an Afrikaans nursery school in Pretoria and grew up able to speak fluent Afrikaans. My DNA has been in Africa for over three hundred years.

What I would love to see Afrikaners do is grow some balls. They have contributed in far greater degree than their share of the population to the arts, sciences, construction, agriculture and technology. I am proud of what Afrikaner there is in me. But for some Afrikaners, none of that makes them feel better.

To give you a good example, I walked into a CD store today and went to the rock section, which I love. On the way I passed three huge racks full of Afrikaans music. I haven't really given it much attention before, but I thought I'd see what was happening …

I'll admit right from the start that I don't listen to Radio Pretoria and I don't speak Afrikaans at home, but I love the language and I love the Afrikaans people with all my heart. What I saw and heard there was, to say the least, rubbish.

I always saw those ads for 'Sokkie Treffers' or 'Suiwer Afrikaans Bokjol Dansklub Gunstelinge' on TV and I thought it was a joke. Turns out they are bona fide records. When did this happen? Who buys this stuff? Clearly there's a market for it, otherwise they could never afford ads in prime time on TV. How is it that this is the best-selling music genre in the country?

Before you think I'm being nasty, consider this: 'Afrikaners feel politically sidelined, globally isolated, culturally compromised and discriminated against in the workplace.' If you don't believe me, believe this: the line you just read was taken from a statement issued by the Vryheidsfront, supported by AfriForum and endorsed by the NG Kerk. So, basically the Afrikaner today is insecure about his place in the world and his future, and is compensating by guiltily supporting his own culture's output, no matter what. Laager mentality.

What happened to the proud, pioneering, inventive, brave men and women who crossed the Drakensberg in their wagons? What happened to the founders of the Republic of South Africa, the people who forged a nation and turned the dry soil into fields of golden maize and ripe fruit? What happened to the culture that gave us CJ Langenhoven's poetry, Eugene Marais' poignant writing, Koos du Plessis's 'Kinders van die Wind' and a people who published newspapers, invented the gun-type nuclear device and, however misguided their policies, stood up to the world? Now, to replace that we have Nicolis Louw and DJ Ossewa. *Ek is teleurgesteld. Wat het met die trotse Afrikaner gebeur?*

If Kortbroek, who is by no means the best example of the Afrikaner male, could have become Minister of Environmental Affairs and Tourism in an ANC government, then just about anybody can get a job.

Ruk julle nou reg. Afrikaners is mos plesierig.

Whine-ex

I made a colossal mistake a few weeks ago, something I will never forgive myself for. I went to WineX. It's an expo for wine and people who like wine.

What a boring waste of time. Picture this: an enormous hall, filled with stands all selling wine. Thousands of people, milling around, looking at bottles, pouring a bit into their glasses, sniffing it, turning it, gargling it, tasting it and mostly spitting it out. I assume the latter was because much of it was rubbish.

According to one of my friends, some people had been there for five or more hours! Can you imagine how devoid of meaning your life has to be before you decide to spend FIVE HOURS with the most pretentious people on earth, sampling something that hasn't changed since the Ancient Egyptians left some grape juice in a jar. What did these people think they were going to find? A cure for cancer?

I like wine at dinner. Truly, some wine is really good. I don't drink red because, nice as it is, it makes me sneeze. I don't really care about the difference between a Chardonnay and a Sauvignon Blanc, but I do know that I can pronounce those two words better than any person I have ever met who is from Cape Town. The fact is that if it costs more than R1 000 a bottle, I probably haven't tasted it. Maybe I'm missing out, maybe not. I'm really not going to get upset about something that will pass through my digestive tract within hours. Of course, some people think the appreciation of expensive wine indicates a refined character. I aver that 750ml of concentrated phosphoric acid costs more than some bottles of wine but it sure as hell won't make me want to taste some.

In case you imagine that I'm being especially unkind to vintners, *sommeliers* and wine connoisseurs, I am not. I reserve an even greater and more especial hatred for TV chefs, and all those who publish cookbooks. The unhealthy attachment of these people (and the ones who watch them and buy their books) to their stomachs usually results in obesity, so I don't have to *actively* discriminate any further when I see them. There is something about bored, spoiled rich people talking about food that I find wasteful.

Since by now I have made myself out to be a complete Philistine, and am probably past saving, let me attempt to balance the scales by admitting that some things are really delicious and that they can, when little else is going on, make taste-memories that last forever. Sometimes I even have the craving to experience them again.

Meals are occasions that lend themselves to all kinds of fun, but the food itself is, from the most cynical point of view, just a source of energy for our mitochondria. Mitochondria are the engines in our cells that make things happen, and they don't really care about the *mousseline* of *pattes rouges* crayfish with morel mushroom infusion that your TV chef showed you how to make. I hate to alienate just about every fat person on earth, but as far as I'm concerned, most meals really are just for nutrition. I'm an 'eat to live' kind of guy, not a 'live to eat' kind. Similarly, the Ancient Romans drank to get drunk, and wine was the cheapest way to do that.

What's in a label?

What do you call yourself? Straight? Gay? Lesbian? Transgender? Bisexual? Transsexual? Asexual? Onanist? Are you Black, Coloured, Mulatto, African, Negro or Brown? Are you Catholic, Presbyterian, Methodist, Lutheran or Greek Orthodox?

Do you have to call yourself anything? Unless you're registering for online dating, the answer is no. In civilised, modern countries in 2011, these labels are about as relevant as your favourite colour or brand of shoe, or preference for Apple or PC. The labels themselves are only relevant to those who define themselves primarily by that label and put their character, personality and spirit after that fact. It is a poor indicator of self-esteem when you describe yourself as a 'single white lesbian South African'. Perhaps you should rather say 'Hi, I'm Mildred and I'd like to buy an angle grinder.'

Someone much wiser than I once said that, if asked to describe yourself, you should always use adjectives rather than nouns or collective nouns. I would rather be described as jovial, intelligent and attractive than white and straight. The latter, rather squalid description gives you information that even Home Affairs could provide and tells you nothing about me. Your race is most important to a racist, your sexuality to a pervert and your nationality to the revenue collector. Tell me about you.

This may not have occurred to all of us, but demographics aren't as interesting as the stories we tell, the things we like, the things we don't. You're probably more likely to have a good time with someone who you think tells funny stories than someone from the same LSM, race, class or gender group as you, right?

Embedded in more rigid societies is the need for people to categorise other people. This process is not just unnecessary in an increasingly multicultural, diverse and colourful world, but also quite destructive. By classifying someone by race, sexuality or nationality, we take the dangerous risk of constructing distasteful stereotypes and prejudices that make it harder, not easier, to really get to know them. For this reason, I am entirely opposed to the idea of these labels. I won't use them any more. It will be difficult, but we have to start somewhere. The terms 'nigger', 'kike' and 'queer' were once considered acceptable, too. Our language must now begin to reflect the better creatures we want to become.

Yes, you're going to die …

Five generations of my family are buried on a hill on family land near Pretoria. Last year we built a wall intended to be the final resting place of my parents, brother, sister, any additions to the family that might still come, and I. When construction of the wall was complete, we packed a picnic basket and all went off to choose our holes in the wall. My mother joked that she wasn't sure she'd like to be too close to my dad. We agreed. He should have the shadiest recess. We drank tea, ate sandwiches and spent the whole afternoon very agreeably. There was no ceremony, austerity or heaviness. I'm sure there will be at some point in the future. I hope I remember the picnic then.

I like to joke about being hit by a bus or eaten by a shark. I'm the guy who boards a plane, looks at the person next to me and thinks, 'Oh no, if we go down, YOU will be the person I share a final moment with', and chuckles. I find death, as a fair certainty, amusing common ground for all of us humans. Those who share this attitude make up only a small number. Most people find death sombre, serious and deeply unfunny.

As something unavoidable, like paying taxes, you'd think we'd have found better ways of coping with the inevitability of death. We joke about taxes, we joke about disasters, but for some reason people always frown when you make some remark about a person dying and then say something like 'It's too soon to be making any fun of that!' Religions have invented afterlife scenarios to help their followers deal with the death of their loved ones. They all talk of paradise, heaven, a place where all will be well for eternity. It helps make people feel better, but they still cry at funerals.

For example, when you read of someone venturing into a swamp and being chomped by a saltwater crocodile, is your first reaction pity or laughter? OK, that might be about 50/50. Here's a better example: when you hear that someone ate a bad steak and shat themselves to death, doesn't it at least make you giggle? It should. Humans sometimes die in interesting ways, and sometimes they're funny. Sometimes it's also OK to laugh at death.

The fact that we're accidentally lucky to exist in the first place seems to be too easily forgotten, and our enormous egos can't deal with how quickly we expire either. Our mortality is an affront to our sense of self-importance. We hate to think about the fact that we're here today and that tomorrow we might be gone, totally and utterly ... gone. That is why some people don't find death funny: they don't see themselves in context.

Here's the context, then: you're in a universe that is about 13.75 billion years old, on a planet that has been around for at least 4.54 billion years. Humans, as far as we would recognise them, have only been roaming the surface of this planet for 150 000 years. The generation gap is about 18 years, and so every 100 years there are about 5.5 generations. Our remotest common human ancestors would have been 8 250 or so generations back. This means that we aren't even a blip on the timeline of the earth, much less the universe; even among mammals we humans and our short lives account for the tiniest fraction of measurable time. To put it plainly, your very temporary presence is not a big deal.

If you think of your 24-hour day as a timeline of the entire history of life on earth, your life would not even fill the amount of time it takes for your brain to send a message to your arm to scratch an itch. Not the scratch, not the duration of the itch, not even the time it takes for the nerve impulse, travelling at 320km/h, to be conducted along its myelinated fibre. The least you can do is have a sense of humour about death – but people don't.

Not so long ago, I attended a funeral for an old man much loved and respected by his family and friends. It was a happy event. People drank and sang, and his grandchildren read out a few stories about their granddad that made us all smile. There was no crying. This man admitted early in his life that he didn't think we were immortal creatures in any way and that the only way we could hope to live on was through our children. Of course he was right, but it takes too many of us too long to come to terms with that. We like thinking we'll be around forever. I've decided I won't leave any assets when I die, so nobody can benefit in any way from my demise.

One day my mortal remains will fill a hole in a wall, and I'm totally OK with that. While I'm alive, laughter brings me much more pleasure than solemnity, and I intend to find reasons to smile in the face of everything, even death.

Old money, new money

It seems in South Africa that we have two kinds of rich: the ones who show they're rich, and the ones who don't. In any given week, some politician's money, cars, houses and expensive clothes come into sharp focus, begging the question of whether they're really rich or just living beyond their means.

These two groups are easier to separate than black from white, old from young and clever from dumb. Can you spot the show-offs? Usually they give you (and SARS) every reason to pick them out from the crowd:

1 They spend more on their cars than their houses

You'll see new German cars parked in townhouse complexes or even cheaper accommodation. Very often the show-off will rent his house so that he can keep that expense (and his numerous other expenses) down and flexible.

2 They have a lot of clothes

and expensive, shiny clothes at that. Often the show-off will have accounts at many clothing stores and will enjoy wearing something only once, even if it costs a fortune. Expensive shoes are a big indicator of status.

3 Their houses are sparsely decorated, if at all

The show-off would rather order fancy drinks at a restaurant, bar or club than entertain at home. This is because he or she never has anything in the fridge or cupboard, and prefers to spend money on instant gratification than on boring furniture or food at home that no-one will see.

4 They always talk about money

They talk about how much things cost, how much they make and how much they plan to make. They exaggerate the amounts out of all proportion.

5 They never pay their bills on time

The show-off uses his credit card or accounts to pay for the instant gratification and worries about paying much, much later. They don't have a problem owing people money. They wait until deadlines have passed, and sometimes never pay at all.

6 They like obvious and ostentatious displays of wealth

(such as watches, bags, sunglasses, phones, flat-screen TVs, jewellery), and not things that have long-term appreciation, like art or books – or even just saving it.

7 They don't arrive on time

They think their time is more valuable than yours, and they want to make a grand (and late) entrance and use it as an opportunity to show off.

Those are just the things I can think of right now – I'm sure you can think of a few more. Really rich people never talk about what they have, how much of it they have or flash it around. They don't have to. Wealth is financial independence and security; it isn't what you have materially.

Beware the crows that collect shiny things. Kleptomania isn't success.

Economy class, economy arse

The good news is rushing to catch your flight and making it, just in time. The bad news is finding yourself in the middle seat. It gets worse. That big man coming down the aisle? He's coming for you.

What is wrong with fat people? Do they lack so much self-control that they just become remorseless eating machines? I'm struggling to type this because I am stuck in economy class on board a two-hour flight to Cape Town, wedged between two Obelixes. Fat Man A is reading a newspaper – not a tabloid-size one, mind you, a full broadsheet spread. Fat Man B had dozed off before we even started to taxi, and his fat banana-shaped fingers keep unlocking over his barrel-shaped belly, resulting in his podgy left arm slipping every two or so minutes and bumping into me.

The sleeping beauty has now begun to snore; his chin has dropped down and his bottom lip has started to gather his spittle, as he makes his way through a nice meat pie in dreamland. My lower ribs are being crushed into the arm of my seat and the flight attendant just made some comment about how they welcome us on board and hope we have a comfortable flight. Nice.

The food trolley is coming. What's the bet he wakes up as soon as he smells something edible? Wait ... Yes! As predicted, he has arisen from his slumber to take the beef, with a Diet Coke. I refuse to eat. I feel sick. I am so uncomfortable that I am now thinking of causing trouble on the plane just so I can be cuffed and taken to the back. Why should I be made to suffer such discomfort when I pay the same price they do for a quarter of the space? I think someone who has lots of money should sue the airlines and force them to have fat flights: they could have benches instead of chairs, serve ice cream, and charge the passengers double.

How can these massive people fool themselves into thinking they can squeeze their gigantic, purulent arses into a small economy-class seat? Stop eating or book yourself into business class, like I do when I have lots of luggage. Speaking of luggage, why do I pay a fine for 'excess baggage', but chubby here weighs as much as four concrete bollards and two packed suitcases and pays the normal fare? It is a crime. Don't give me that nonsense about human rights and all people being equal, because I could fit into this man twice and he'd still squeeze in a Happy Meal.

Fat Man B's featureless bottom of a face is now tilting to the left, probably because his bloated head has become heavy – either that or his neck rolls have moved. The only part of his face that has not expanded to accommodate adipose tissue is the area around his temples. Otherwise, he looks like a cartoon character, except he isn't making me laugh. As soon as he has demolished his beef sandwich, he is off to sleep again. His snoring has now become regular – and nice and loud. He has also decided that it's no longer worth pretending to keep his pigs' trotters clasped over his mammoth frame, and has just let his arms slump all the way over me. They are hot and moist and are making me feel worse.

I've sat next to screaming babies, people who sneeze their filthy germs all over the cabin, old ladies who stink of wee, and even a woman in the USA who made her own sardine sandwiches on her tray table between New York and Los Angeles, but I have never been so uncomfortable with the state of humanity. You are what you eat, and I give fat people a hard time because I don't want to lose a listener, and the fat ones are at greatest risk. We all know that obesity is one of the leading causes of death, and we are all responsible for our own health.

I just had a thought: if they want to put graphic pictures of diseased lungs and corroded hearts on cigarette packs to frighten people who smoke too much, shouldn't they put a picture of Khulubuse Zuma on every box of doughnuts? At least they'd be consistent.

Tarts

I have always had a soft spot for tarts. They aren't a great threat to humanity (in fact, they do rather a lot relating to the survival of the species), they keep the glamour industry alive, and they watch reality TV. Tarts are good value at parties and they're cheap dates – they don't eat much. However, when the atmosphere dies down and you're faced with each other and no other distractions, a tart can be very difficult to communicate with. Unless you're talking about her, she won't be very interested in talking at all. So what can you do?

Well, you can't play 30 Seconds or Trivial Pursuit. She won't enjoy rough shows like Bear Grylls or war programmes on the History Channel. Tarts aren't good at touch rugby or garden cricket, and you can't joke with them because they have very fragile egos and will think every joke is at their expense, even ones about building materials and Aborigines. You can't leave them with an iPad in a corner of the room and tell them to surf the net because their fake nails render them unable to operate a touch screen effectively. You see, you're stuck when it comes to anything more than attempting to get them to go home with you.

If you have a tart in your life, she will need to do things while you get on with your actual job. She can't be left unsupervised at home because she will rearrange furniture, leave a cigarette burning on some flammable surface, or burn to a crisp in the sun. Here are a list of things she could do for money: she could be a low-level receptionist, a beautician, a hairdresser, a model, a dancer, a pop star, a stripper, a cheerleader, a cigarette promoter or a reality TV star. If she's ambitious, she might work for a magazine, decorate someone else's home or go to the shops for you.

In their spare time, tarts have complex relationships with their cellphones, which are usually decorated with fake diamonds or other shiny things.

They can spend hours and hours on them, during which time you needn't bother talking to them at all. They will usually chew gum and look at their nails while talking on the phone. Try not to be put off. You can leave the house during this time, meet an old friend, have a drink – even a meal – and they won't notice that you've gone. When you come back, eight days later, they'll still be on the phone.

If your tart seems bored, or her phone battery or the soap operas have run out, you'll need to give her money. She will spend said money on clothing, jewellery, handbags and shoes, in a never-ending accumulation cycle. Be warned: she will also buy many glossy magazines. By the time you get home, tired from work, she will need to be let out for exercise.

At night, tarts enjoy the company of a few like-mindless girls and some complete strangers in bars and nightclubs. Here they will drink sweet alco-pops and other horrible drinks until they get cross-eyed and/or tired. This is the customary 'golden hour' when a tart is at her most useful. She will sleep with you and then pass out.

And so it is that tarts find their place in the circle of life. The golden hour makes up for all the annoying, pointless consumer existence that fills up the other hours of her day. While you and I marvel at the minds of Hawking, Einstein, Voltaire and Chesterton, she gasps at the wisdom of the Kardashians. God bless the tart.

You be the judge

According to the ANC Youth League in Limpopo, I'm a madman, a backward-thinking, ultra-right-winger, biased against people over the age of 28.

I am obviously mad, so I won't fight them on that front. The rest I can't agree with.

The source of all the ANCYL Limpopo's anguish was an offhand comment I made to the *Sunday Times* about *Idols* and the lack of talent in Polokwane. It was a true statement. There was a dismal smattering of some very average singing ability, with only one guy who was really talented. One guy! And he wasn't even from Polokwane. He worked out that he would stand more chance if he auditioned in Poloks than in Jo'burg, and it worked! We travelled all the way there, at enormous cost, with a TV crew of more than 50 people. What a waste of time.

Since they brought it up, let's look at Limpopo province – because it never gets any attention. Limpopo has the lowest matric pass rate out of all the provinces. They have the least number of university graduates. Limpopo has a declining provincial economy, and its only claim to fame is the number of mentions in the *Daily Sun* newspaper – more than any other province – usually in stories related to the *tokoloshe* or bestiality. The ANCYL in Limpopo are the ones who, famously, locked out half their own members from their pants-dropping elective conference in 2010, and under the most suspicious circumstances elected their current leader. Let me add all of these attributes to 'untalented' before we close the book on Limpopo province.

As with any other place, there are probably some very intelligent, interesting people in Polokwane and the rest of Limpopo province. The full quote from the *Sunday Times* read as follows (and this is me speaking, referencing *Idols* auditions): 'The people in Polokwane are charming, but not very talented.' I stand by this comment. Everyone we met was both those things, and remember we didn't meet *everyone* in Polokwane. Had we met the ANCYL there, I may have used one less adjective.

Haven't you ever said something offhand that didn't even matter much to you when you said it? That's what happened here. This is why I'm sometimes branded a 'shock jock' and 'loudmouth', among other terms of endearment. This is a good example. I was doing what a judge does and pronouncing judgment. It is my job on *Idols* to say what I think of the talent. Unlike the ANCYL in Limpopo, most of whom probably wouldn't know talent if it jumped out of their Rice Krispies and bit them, I have a basic standard I like to apply when judging people – and it has absolutely nothing to do with race. Since the ANCYL Limpopo insist on dragging this debate into the sandpit, I will join them just long enough to hand them a little plastic spade and insist they keep on digging, and hope too that the Bible is correct in saying: 'He that diggeth a pit, shall surely fall into it' (Proverbs 26:27).

Julius Malema called me on Sunday night after the show aired. He was laughing. All he could say was: 'You're right, there's no talent in Polokwane.' So Juju does make sense sometimes.

Who wants to live forever?

Do you want to live forever? Futurist and scientist Ray Kurzweil thinks that if we're able to live another 20 or so years, we'll live long enough to live forever. He reckons that with the improvements in science and medicine, the exponential increase in what we know and how much we still can know, we'll be able to push longevity to new outer limits. In the future, small mechano-synthesising nanobots will construct, reconstruct and destroy proteins, hormones, impurities and mutated strands of DNA and replace whole unhealthy cells. According to Kurzweil, within the next 20 years we will have reverse-engineered the brain and our ability to understand and more fully utilise it will be complete.

The question I'm sure you're asking is whether this is a future you'll want.

There are a few things you'll need to get used to. Let's start with daily routines. Eating won't be the same; you'll swallow a pill or two for nutrition, but tasting things will become a completely sensory experience. You won't have to ingest a fatty lamb chop to have the satisfaction of eating one. Your brain will be tricked into the experience, electronically. But have no fear; sushi from Nobu will be on the menu every night, even in horrible little mining towns.

Sleep will be optional, since the nanobots will do all the repair and reconstruction work while you're busy doing things yourself, so a 24-hour day will become entirely realistic. So your boss will be able to send you urgent e-mails at 3am. No pressure …

You will no longer need the loo. This is a very satisfactory thought. In the future, any waste inside your body will be utilised and converted long before it needs to be expelled. In fact, it will be converted at molecular level into usable constituent parts. Imagine not having to suffer the indignity of public lavatories and all the associated foul smells and filth. For no other reason, I say bring on the future. Although there will always be arseholes, we may not actually ever need them again.

Sex will be much enhanced. Actual, physical contact will probably remain, but sex will happen in binary. You'll be able to sleep with a Kardashian, a French maid, or both, without even moving from the sofa. There needn't ever again be an uncomfortable morning after, filled with guilt, regret or the danger of venereal disease.

Your appearance will be enhanced, and youthfulness will be entirely programmable. No wrinkles, no liver spots, no baldness, no loss of eyesight or deterioration of function. Your muscles will be optimised, your organs revitalised and your skin smoothed and uniform. To put it plainly, you'll look your best every day, all day. Physicians will no longer have stethoscopes and wooden tongue depressors; they'll have wireless scanning devices and upgrade packs to install.

Imagine a world where you won't need to spend hours memorising information, where everything will be instantly recalled from a powerful indexing and storage neurological library, where a Harvard, UCT or Oxford degree upgrade will be readily available. All of this, the cleverest people say, is almost a reality.

So what could the downside possibly be? Well, you'd have to abandon the idea of growing old, running out of time, planning your life according to the clock humanity has used for the last ten thousand years. This may not seem like a big ask, but we're not used to being around for as long as we one day might. You'll have to get your head around great-great-great-grandchildren, much bigger family gatherings. Marriages are unlikely to last for a hundred years, and age will not be important, so you might have a 200-year-old boyfriend. Being beautiful, clever, fast or sexy will distinguish us less and less from each other and our personalities will be the biggest difference between us. A sense of humour, it seems likely, will remain individual and unalterable.

You'll also have to give up on an afterlife. First of all, you won't need one; second, that option will not be a logical possibility any more. If we are in absolute control of our destiny, there really isn't any reasonable room for a god. In the future, the old scriptures will be even more irrelevant than they are now. I'm afraid it may be the end of the supernatural and of most mystery.

Some fear that the robots may take over. I have some bad news: they already have. Computers are now reprogramming themselves, changing their source code without instruction and improving their functionality, efficiency and adaptation to the environment. Computer programmers won't have work in a few years. The computers will take over from them. Ethical and moral considerations will have to be injected into the rules to keep computers working for us. There will be challenges, but hopefully no Terminators.

If you're reading this now, your future could be just as I've described it. Until then, you'll need good health and some money to make it there. Just live long enough, and make sure you're rich enough to hit 2025. For the poor, the future is exactly the same as the present, I'm afraid. I can't wait to date your great-great-granddaughter.

Your boring life

How do you feel about celebrities? Aren't you tired of them? I don't look up to them, and I'm not interested in photographs of them all dressed up.

Do you understand tabloids either? Everything about them is at least a bit rotten: the pictures of flabby stars on the beach, the stories of broken Hollywood relationships, and the fashion faux pas of the elite. The sum total of their literary content (if I can be allowed, in good conscience, to call it that) would amount to no more than a page or two of solid script. So who 'reads' this schlock?

Hate to break it to you, but the average tabloid reader isn't famous, rich or attractive. Oh, they like to read about the famous, rich and attractive people, but not really because they like them. When John Bradford, the English religious reformer and martyr, said, while watching a prisoner being led to his execution, 'There, but for the grace of God, go I,' what he really meant was 'There, but for the grace of God, goes someone else.' It's *schadenfreude*, a German word for the pleasure we derive from the misfortune of others. It's also the reason fat, ugly, un-famous people read tabloids. I think it's also very unhealthy.

I picked up a copy of one of these magazines a while ago to see if things had improved – you know, since the Large Hadron Collider had begun to smash protons and since we discovered the gene that leads to macular degeneration. No such luck. The headlines were about one of the Kardashians getting fat, Streisand's next last-ever tour, Brad Pitt growing a beard and John Travolta getting drunk with a group of unsavoury sex workers in a sauna. The less interesting you are, it seems, the more interesting everyone else becomes.

It's the same thing with a royal wedding. Old ladies without teeth in remote Cumbrian cottages cannot help themselves when it comes to buying wheelbarrows full of nasty, tacky memorabilia. They have Will and Kate hand towels, pillows, thimbles and clocks. Is it a lack of personal happiness that makes the marriage of two complete strangers a valid reason to feel excited? They watch reruns of Prince Charming walking down the aisle with his beaming (and, I have to say, quite sexy) Princess. It's like when someone loses a pet but keeps their basket and collar in the entrance hall to remind themselves of how things might have been. Psychologists must look into this.

The royal wedding was actually a very entertaining spectacle, a news event, but not something we needed to skip work for. Or was it? I suppose some people have such monotonous lives that this was a respite, a break from the chill of reality. Are we nasty if we begrudge them this? Surely the only point of celebrities is that they offer this value to ordinary people? I really don't know.

The tabloid is a steamy window through which the reader may catch a tiny glimpse of the sexy and exciting world of the stars they admire from a distance. It's voyeurism writ large ... And while I'm at it, reality TV, which is a moving-picture tabloid, fulfils the same need for those too lazy to read.

I wonder what a gossip magazine would contain if it were only allowed to tell the stories of its own readers: 'Bertha buys sausages!'; 'Tina lights her farts!'; 'Dennis – still big and fat!' I doubt you'd buy it. The need for some human mammals to watch the uninteresting activities of other human mammals means that some of us just have too much time on our hands, or a desperate need to fantasise. If you ever find yourself bored and rifling through a magazine, do the honourable thing and buy an actual book, and stop the de-evolution of the species while you still can.

To catch a cheat

Have you ever cheated on someone? Have you ever been caught? Perhaps you had someone cheat on you? Maybe you suspect there's cheating going on right now ...

I'm not the first person to ask these questions, and I'm sure you've thought about them a hundred times – even if you have the perfect relationship. We primates have a tough time walking the line between the instinct to nurture families and our young on the one hand, and the drive to give in to temptation on the other. When I'm confused by a question about behaviour, I look either to the elevated and wise among my own species, or to the ways of coarse, unyielding nature. The answers are always diametrically opposed: nature suggests abandoning social, religious and political constructs and giving in to base desires. The wisest men and women will always say that the physical must be mastered for greater reward in the mental, emotional and spiritual dimensions. So which do you choose to trust and follow? Is it not a delicate balancing act that can precariously slip either way if you don't monitor it carefully?

To say one is wrong and the other right is dangerous, too. Too many episodes in history have been played out by either set of rules, producing very different outcomes. If Henry VIII hadn't been such a philanderer, would there ever have been a Reformation in England? Everywhere we look, cheating impacts heavily on the immediate families concerned, the community and sometimes even the country, so we should, at the very least, take affairs seriously.

I don't like cheating. I believe that when you meet someone who appeals to you more than the person you're with you should be man (or woman) enough to end the existing relationship before moving on to another one, especially if you have some kind of long-term arrangement with that person. To keep that person in the dark, or attempt to have your cake and eat it, is ethically problematic, to say the least. What you're really saying is that the cheated-upon party isn't worthy of the same degree of decency, honesty or value as you. Not on at all.

Whether we're monogamous creatures or not isn't my concern; if you choose to be with someone, and that relationship means something, you can't go round the town being with other people. If you choose to be single and play around with other people, then don't be in a relationship. They are non-overlapping magisteria. You must apply logic to the situation objectively to determine your values before entering the relationship and potentially becoming subjective.

Not every relationship has the same rules, but dishonesty can only lead to misery. Surely the most painful part of the cheating process is the pain that is brought about by deceit. Would you agree?

I suppose some sort of all-encompassing solution is possible, like polygamy or the delicate balancing act of an 'open relationship', but I have yet to hear of one of the latter that doesn't end in tears, or one of the former that isn't a nightmare to manage.

My grandfather used to say: 'Be nice to people.' It's a good philosophy. No matter what you call it, cheating isn't nice.

If the truth be told

There are some things people say that just aren't true. They are, however, mostly due to repetition, taken at face value and considered as facts. Here are some examples.

1 A good education can make an ignorant person clever

Nonsense. Cast your mind back to when you were at school. There were clever kids and stupid kids. Exposed to the exact same syllabus, books, teachers and examinations, some of these kids emerged as clever and some remained stupid. Same education, different results. As Forrest Gump said, 'Stupid is as stupid does,' whatever that means …

2 Violence in movies begets violence in real life

Bullshit. Just because Jason Bourne shoots, kicks, stomps and punches everyone on screen doesn't mean that little 82-year-old Mrs Nhlengethwa is suddenly going to arm up and exterminate the townsfolk after exiting the theatre. Conversely, if it were true that aggressive movies or video games led to real-life aggression, then why is incest such a massive societal problem, despite virtually no acknowledgement of this malady by Hollywood?

3 If a poor person wins the lottery, their life will change forever

Rubbish. Statistically, most people who have no money and win the lottery end up just as poor a few years after their win. This is because they never understood money to start with, and winning a whole lot of it didn't change that. They had a big dinner in America last year for all the living Lotto winners. Most of them are poorer now than they were before they won. Poor isn't always poor because you don't have; poor is sometimes poor because you can't make.

4 You can practise and train and become a great singer, actor or dancer

Bollocks. Talent is either there or it isn't. No amount of training can make a tone-deaf singer fantastic. Of course, training can make a talented person even better, but it will do nothing for the person who has none to begin with. Basically, you can't polish a turd.

5 'If you believe it, you can achieve it'

Lies. This may work as a lyric for R Kelly – when he isn't molesting underage girls – but in real life it isn't true. I might believe with all my heart that I am a world-class footballer, but that brings me not a scintilla closer to actually becoming one. Oprah and Dr Phil are wrong: you are not a treasure-trove of undiscovered potential; you're only the best *you* can be – and sometimes that's really ordinary.

6 Legalising drugs will increase drug abuse

Untrue! In the few open-minded places on earth where drugs are not illegal, the vast majority of people there are not druggies and vacuous potheads. They also don't have jails full of minor offenders and they don't have a nasty underground economy, ruled by thugs and pimps. People who want drugs will get them, either from illegal dealers, or, less dangerously, across the counter of a licensed supplier. The law is of little interest to someone who is addicted, and it certainly plays no part in making non-users into users, or vice versa.

7 Guns kill people

Crap. People kill people. If someone wants to kill, a gun will merely make his job easier. If he can't find a gun, he'll use a knife, cardboard cutter or swizzle stick. Eliminating guns from the equation puts potential victims at a greater disadvantage, and changes nothing for the murderer except his choice of tool.

8 Tobacco advertising makes non-smokers want to start smoking

Trash. Most people who start smoking do so because they want to, because someone they know pressures them into it, or because they think it's cool. Wonderful as tobacco advertising used to be, it was nowhere near as sexy as a Wonderbra ad is now. Even so, seeing a Wonderbra ad doesn't make me want to wear women's clothing. Similarly, as a non-smoker, I have never driven past a cigarette billboard and thought, 'Oh yeah, that convinced me! Better stop at the next tobacconist and stock up on cancer sticks.'

9 Prostitution should be illegal because it is immoral

Kak! Prostitution shouldn't matter to people who call themselves moral. It matters to everyone else, though. It's the oldest and most popular profession. For the same reason that underground drug use is destructive, making hookers afraid of the law makes the hookers themselves less safe. The law will not stop a horny old married man from paying a woman to have sex with him. If you can't stop politicians from doing it, why punish the hookers? Be honest and admit you just don't like other people having sex for money, because your sex life is no fun and feels like work.

10 All children are innocent, beautiful creatures

Please! Some children are nasty, vicious little monsters who dismember family pets and actively destroy the possessions of adults. They also scream on planes, urinate and defecate at will, and cost their parents a fortune. The only people who can't be objective about this fact are parents themselves.

Next time someone spouts one of these statements of profound wisdom, please promise me you'll tell them they're full of it. Question everything, especially the stuff they tell you is gospel … Even gospel isn't.

Many ways to skin a cat

I love animals. Earlier this year I got a new puppy. His name is Carl. I know what you're thinking: that's not a dog's name. Dogs have personalities just like humans do. Carl loves his name. We've always had dogs and cats. There was a stage, on the farm, when we had dogs, cats, rabbits, pigeons, horses and chickens, among other animals.

Sadly, my sister's cat Sox had to be put down this year after 20 years of ruling the house. I put an obituary on Facebook for Sox, which received an outpouring of commiseration. Pets hold a special place in many families' hearts and homes. As invariably happens on our Facebook conversations, however, one comment can unleash a deluge of deap-seated racism.

Sipho joined the Sox tribute, and commented that in his culture cats are considered to be *tokoloshe*, and that black people are taught to kill them on sight. He continued that it's lucky he didn't meet Sox before or we would have been mourning much sooner! I found this comment honest and amusing. Clearly not everyone shares this sense of humour or appreciates a different perspective. Who knew that a dead cat could cause such a row?

Poor Sipho came under scathing attack from angry white people, and even some black folk who thought he was giving them a bad name. Sox's tribute turned into a bitter racial slanging match. Sipho tried to explain that he didn't mean to be disrespectful, but that is what he was taught. I acknowledged his comment with appreciation (yes, I do read the comments), but the offended parties blindly bulldozed on, clinging to the racial accusations.

If you live in South Africa, and you've never been called a racist, you probably don't say much. You may have noticed a tendency for people to imagine, not unreasonably, that everything in South Africa has to do with race. The simplest fool knows that the mere allegation of racism carries with it the greatest degree of pain, guilt, suffering and humiliation. The bad news is that racism cannot be totally eradicated. Even within races, people find reasons to discriminate. It all comes down to the unfortunate reality of our pattern-seeking mammalian brains and their tendency to generalise at every opportunity.

One thing about Facebook: people who join the public conversations seem to be more comfortable saying things that they wouldn't say face-to-face. A degree of anonymity allows for civility to be suspended, while deep-seated anger and insecurities ooze out like pus being squeezed from a boil. At one time I honestly thought that we were beyond this, and that it was only the older generation that carried baggage from the past. It's tremendously saddening when I post something on Facebook that I think is funny only for it to yield a racial backlash. On the other hand, this could be the forum that genuinely allows the deap-seated poison to surface and, in time, facilitate our coming to a place of more openness to our colourful multicultural society and acceptance of the richness of our diversity.

Often, racism has more to do with the way you feel about yourself than anything the other person has said or done. Those who imagine themselves always to be victims will undoubtedly jump to the conclusion that everyone is out to get them. Their own insecurity may spur the use of the race card far quicker than any insult ever could.

Calling someone a racist invariably ends any possibility of engaging in fruitful discussion. If someone cries racism, then it must be so. Usually the other party is so irredeemably damaged by the accusation that they also lose the will to defend themselves, even if there are no grounds for playing the card in the first place. It is a frustrating impasse.

Since the charge brings such destructive finality to any human communication, we must avoid it unless we see absolutely no other way to deal with a bigot. Perception in this case, as ever, is everything. Before calling out the racist, make sure you have no need or desire to ever interact with that human again, because it will be impossible to do so once the accusation is made.

So Sipho, I'm also glad that you didn't meet Sox and make him the front page *tokoloshe* story for the *Daily Sun*. I understand that cats as pets was not part of your upbringing, and may even have been part of your diet. That doesn't make you a racist. There's many ways to skin a cat. No self-respecting contrarian should ever be the first to call someone else a racist.

The fall of the British Empire

Kay Burley, that saucy newsreader on Sky News, revealed something extra stupid the other day. It seems that British culture has started plumbing ever-greater depths of depravity: according to Kay, a 13-year-old boy recently became a father. I don't know too much about the circumstances or details, mostly because I was so shocked that I choked and had to rush out of the room.

You read that right the first time: a 13-year-old! He is quoted as saying: 'I looove me sooon and I know I'm gon' be a goood fathur,' or something like that. Kay's comment was: 'Can a 13-year-old live up to his promise to be a good father?' What a lovely politically correct question, Kay! Of course he can't! There cannot be a 'yes' answer to Kay's question, no matter how sensually she poses it, even with those pouty lips and bedroom eyes. He's 13! If his parents help, he's not being a good father, his father is; and since he can neither get a job or go to school if he intends being a good father, he hands his child a poisonous and bleak future, fraught with confusion and poverty, and heaps life-inexperience on stupidity.

This child of 13 should have been sterilised, and his girlfriend forced to have an abortion, not by government but by their families. If their families refused, the community should have razed their council house to the ground and dragged the children off to the clinic, bearing pitchforks and burning torches. What happened to common sense? We no longer have the excuses of ignorance or lack of information with which to defend such craven irresponsibility. These children have, by their actions, shown that they will be unlikely to make any contribution to the society of Britain or the world. They will eat, breathe, fart and fuck. Until they stop. They have crossed a line by bringing another living human being into this cycle of senselessness, and there ought to be consequences for them.

Let me explain the complex relationship I have with Britain, or more especially England, because that's the country I'm talking about. My ancestors come overwhelmingly from there. Of my 16 great-great-grandparents, only five were not born in England. Deeper into my family history are people who, from as early as AD 400 started forging the nation of the English. I still have, and always will have, an abiding, deep and powerful connection to the place. On the occasions I have been there, I have been there for the history of it, not for the people who inhabit it now. There is an inexplicable familiarity with all things English, as if by a collective genetic memory I should know the place as well as I know the African bush – but I don't. I don't feel at home there; the sky feels low and the light is dim. There isn't (although some may disagree) much of modern England in me any more. I am thoroughly African. It's just as well.

Britain has become a really horrible country. Here are two examples that illustrate the problem. First of all, in June this year, a woman was caught harbouring her mother's dead corpse, which she was keeping propped up behind a door in a flat, while for six months she continued to claim monthly benefits of £200. She kept a rotten corpse in her house and siphoned £200 out of the state rather than go out and find employment. This has to be a new level of laziness.

A few weeks before that, the papers carried the story of a fat family on welfare who were bemoaning the fact that they didn't get enough in benefits from the state. The two fat daughters couldn't be pushed to exercise because they're too busy eating, and the father was actually quoted as saying: 'We love TV. Sometimes I get so tired of watching TV that I need to take a nap.' They don't like healthy food because of the taste, so they eat pies, takeaways and chocolate.

These are the sort of people who have turned the once-mighty British Empire into a pig's trough, where someone like Jade Goody could rise to prominence. Do you remember Jade? She was the racist *Celebrity Big Brother* contestant who made derogatory remarks about Bollywood actress Shilpa Shetty. Since then she went on to do just about everything she could to remain in the tabloids and on TV. She even wanted to die on TV. The cameras, thankfully, stopped just short of granting her request.

Jade, the corpse-keeper, the fat family and the 13-year-old dad are signs that Britain is in terrible decline. Succeeding generations will be incompetent, uneducated yobs lacking in ambition and overflowing with misplaced overconfidence. Already they stab each other in schools and torment grannies in quiet streets. Civil obedience isn't even something that crosses their minds – and their nanny-state government will continue to coddle them until the nation collapses.

As I write this, I break to glance at that old trout Kay Burley, just in time to see that riots have broken out all over London, as well as in Birmingham, Liverpool and other cities. Gangs of teenage chavs are wandering around, setting fire to shops, breaking windows and looting with violence, abandon and malice. Poor Boris Johnson, the mayor of London, has had to cut his holiday short to come back and take control of the streets. A professor from Liverpool University appears on TV and says the reason the 'youths' are stealing high-end goods is because the wealth gap is too large and they feel excluded from the rich people in society and all their luxuries. What a disgraceful apologist and idiot. If that man can be a professor, then I'm manning the mission to Mars. These kids are nothing but greedy criminals without any discipline or direction. They have no respect for authority and no desire to achieve anything by themselves. They want it all, and they want it now – and if you won't give it to them, they'll take it by force. This is the terminus to which political correctness, banal multiculturalism, left-wing soft psychology and social welfare have brought us. We are witnessing the final fall of the British Empire. It won't go out with a bang; it will just fizzle and fade away.

These children are the offspring of parents who got everything the welfare state could dole out to them. They were not discriminated against because they were poor, nor because they were stupid, nor because they had run away from their own rubbish countries before coming to England, nor because they couldn't get a job. The British government said they'd help them, and they did. Now they just help themselves.

Stupid is as stupid does

Do you get the feeling there are a lot of really stupid people around? Have you ever looked at someone and thought 'Was that really the fastest sperm to make it to the egg?'

Some time ago on a plane to Cape Town we were delayed because some stupid woman was wandering around the airport buying chocolates and things while the rest of us and her bags were already aboard. They had to track her down because we couldn't fly with her baggage and without her. I don't see why we couldn't just drop them into the sea before we landed.

That woman is stupid because all she had to remember was to get on to the plane, and she couldn't. She should never be allowed to fly again. I shudder to think what someone so stupid needs to do in Cape Town anyway – it can't be important. Next time she can walk, or take a bus.

If you really think it's about education, let me set you straight. People have been getting no, or at least unequal, education for years. Only recently have some countries managed to give their citizens any kind of basic education. So before the 20th century, if you believe it's all about education, most people were stupid. Many of the greatest figures of the Enlightenment would take issue with you, as will I.

Stupid people have been among us, and will continue to be, for many centuries. At school I knew a kid who actually seemed to get dumber the more education he got … He used to carve his initials incorrectly into the wood of his school desk, and brawl with smaller kids during break. Once, when a teacher reprimanded him for eating the pages of his textbook, this mouth-breather did his best to muster the profound words 'It's maaa laaaf' (It's my life) before being sent outside. It was true that it was his life, but what a life. This poor boy is probably desecrating churches and knifing pensioners to buy drugs as you read this. It could all have been stopped if we had just caught his parents and paid them not to make him. Being stupid themselves, they'd probably have preferred the money anyway.

In the old days, simple, natural laws of survival kept stupid people's numbers down – you know, they'd fall asleep in the savanna under trees and get eaten by lions, or their shoddily constructed houses would fall in on them, or they'd be consumed by the volcano on whose slopes they'd settled. In ancient times, war and disease took their toll on the numbers, and the arrow fodder in the front lines of any battle were usually the dimmest soldiers. The clever, fast, fit ones fought better and harder and survived. These days, the dim ones last longer – thanks to democracy, welfare and liberal humanitarianism (that ridiculous school of thinking that treasures human life, even stupid human life, above all). Luckily, thanks to modern conveniences, some still manage to eliminate themselves: electric appliances fall into the bath, they cross highways on foot, and eat food that clogs their arteries. Unfortunately, stupid people still out-breed clever people, but at least they can afford to lose a few from their number.

If you haven't seen the movie *Idiocracy* (2006), watch it. It's not a great movie, but it will make you think. It's a story about how dumb people take over the world. Humans are the only creatures that seem to actively fight the basic laws of survival. In other words, we're the only species that keeps bad genes in circulation. It means one thing: de-evolution. We're not adapting positively. We're not improving as a group of natural animals. How long do you think we'll last?

Sex, sex ... and more sex

God gave men both a penis and a brain, but unfortunately not enough blood supply to run both at the same time. — Robin Williams

You've heard all about Tiger Woods, Michael Douglas, Bill Clinton, poor Anthony Weiner and Charlie Sheen. All of them, we are led to believe, suffer from some kind of sex addiction. Well, that's what the shrinks say ... I thought all of nature had a sex addiction, and that precisely was responsible for the continuation of the species. But maybe I'm wrong, and the psychologists have found a new way to make money.

The sex addiction that the aforementioned poontang-crazed gentlemen have is apparently curable. This is especially good news for Clinton and Douglas, who would by now be not just dirty old men, but very dirty, very old men. Many of these horn-dogs can now seek help in sex addiction treatment centres across America. That's all we know – that these places exist. What I'd like to know is how they actually treat skirt-chasing leches like Tiger Woods and David Letterman. Do you know what goes on in there?

For our own amusement, let's imagine what happens in these treatment centres. They're probably like fat farms or spas, with a difference: gruff, objectively hideous staff punish you if you even smile at them. Treatments likely include pacing up and down the corridors, cold showers, a Lily Tomlin film festival, and asparagus at every meal. Every evening at the House of Guilt, shame and ridicule are poured upon you by the eunuch guru, Sri Bagawan Cohen. Recordings of your wife complaining are played while you try to sleep, alternating with periods of her refusing to even speak to you, also on tape. During the day at no-sex boot camp, they promise they haven't gone soft but remind you that you surely will. In the draconian sex-averse lodge for serial offenders, manly retired gym teacher Norma 'Coach' Hinkel plays the part of an appropriately unyielding harpy. Here, with force, she will teach you to become a sexless, new-age drone. Portraits of notorious anti-arousal legends Eleanor Roosevelt, Barbara Bush, Camilla Parker-Bowles, Nkosazana Dlamini-Zuma and Mrs Doubtfire adorn the walls. Can you imagine?

Just the thought of such a place would cure even our super-horny President. Either that or a rerun of the sterile *Girls of the Playboy Mansion*, which seems to have taken the sexy right out of *Playboy* and replaced it with the sunset of a sad old Viagra addict and his brainless, parasitic daughterly companions.

Damagement

Where have all the leaders gone? The crisis of leadership is bad enough, but there is also a void that is filled by managers – people trying to control. Like robots, but without the artificial intelligence that makes robots more or less infallible, they find a place in the corporate hierarchy and stay as long as they can. I've never studied the theory of management, but I think everyone knows that Peter Drucker is one of the gurus in this field. He said: 'So much of what we call management consists in making it difficult for people to work.'

With my short attention span, that's as far as my formal education in management goes, but I understand why they call him a guru. Do any of these theories of management really matter? Does e-mail upon e-mail of rules and regulations really accomplish anything, especially when everyone in the business is copied on every detail of everyone else's correspondence? I do sympathise with some managers because they have to put up with incessant moaning and blaming, but having said that, they ask for it.

Managers seem to turn into their parents or teachers or ministers – pray here, kneel there, break this, don't break that, do this, don't do that. I don't react well to that sort of authoritarian control. Not many of us do. We all know what kids are like with authority figures, and I feel a tantrum coming on …

Since I started hosting the breakfast show on 5FM five years ago, I've been through four general managers, four station managers, four programme managers, several 'acting' managers and an indeterminate number of suspended executives in the upper echelons, many of whom had their hands so deep in the till that they had to be surgically separated from it. Each new set of managers brings less experience and more procedures and processes. Have you noticed how management is forever having strategy sessions? The best strategy is to go and do your bloody work, no?

Perhaps the process of controlling things and people is beneficial in some businesses, but surely this is only useful if you don't need creativity and ingenuity. That's what most people bring to the table, and you can't extract it by creating yet another process, procedure or plan. Can you imagine (and you probably can), some middle manager saying: 'Our strategy is that you will come up with something brilliant.' It doesn't work that way.

No matter who you are or what job you have, you're going to have to answer to some sort of managerial monster. They could be great fiery dragons with low EQs, brandishing a whip to extract your sweat for every cent they loathingly pay you. They could be effete, incompetent dullards who attained their position by connections, a paucity of talent or just hanging around until all the better people were gone. Your manager could even be the worst kind of person – the one who wants to be everyone's friend. I'm learning how to deal with all the different types of authority, and I like none of them. Hard as it may be to exercise self-control with these sorts of people, it's often the only way to make the inconvenience go away, and just avoiding them can actually make you feel better than a good interaction with them.

The Metro cops have given me plenty of experience. Don't you hate it when you're cruising down the highway, swiftly but peacefully, and a shrieking siren shatters your reverie, and the blue lights bear down on you. Bust! Cops can be susceptible to corruption, they can abuse their power, and they can be irrational, but *you've* broken the law. Whatever you may be bust for, the only thing you can do is smile and make nice. More often than not, you'll get out of more tickets by complimenting them on their smart uniforms and shiny badges than you will by arguing your case for speeding. Tell them how right they are to put you in your place. It's the exact opposite of what most people tell them. Most of the time, they'll be so blown away they'll give you a warning and let you go. But you have to take the ticket. If you offer them a bribe, then you're perpetuating the corruption problem that plagues our country. Man up.

The same logic applies to SARS. The only thing in life you can be sure of is death and paying tax. I don't like having to give a sizeable chunk of my earnings to SARS. In fact, there is nothing that eases the pain of paying tax. It breaks my heart that so much of the money I have worked so hard to gather unto myself should be so wantonly and wastefully apportioned to a greedy tenderpreneur or a fat female MP who needs a new, towering hat. It's perverse, but you must pay up.

'The boss' – and that could be a collective (you know, safety in numbers) – is the one creature of authority we have to deal with on a daily basis. This one can, however, be more easily circumvented. Smile and do your work. Do it for yourself, not them, but let them think it's all about them. Be mindful, though, that there will come a day when you will no longer be able to hold your tongue and keep your smile. Make sure, on that day, that it's worth it.

Management or damagement? Which do you have? Today our work ethics and corporate belief systems are totally different to those experienced by older generations. We have access to information on a scale that nobody could have imagined even ten years ago, and we have thousands of friends on Facebook and other social networking sites. Our networks are larger and more varied than ever before. We have a bigger frame of reference and we don't spend our whole day toiling at the office, trying to make friends with people we would never choose to associate with outside of work. Managers can't control you any more, particularly when you can look up something on Google and explain to them why they're wrong before they even have a chance to correct themselves.

We will not be 'managed'. Hire the best, pay them properly, and allow them to do what they do best. Coach and mentor by all means, but don't try and fit square pegs into round holes. This whole thing reminds me of something brilliant Paul Dickson once said: 'Never try to teach a pig to sing; it wastes your time and it annoys the pig.'

Lock 'n load

Do you own a gun? Are you scared of guns? Maybe you've seen what they can do and you're frightened. That's OK; it doesn't make you weak, but maybe you should read this before you give anyone an uneducated opinion on guns.

I own a licensed gun. I am proud of being a gun owner. I would own many more guns if it weren't so very tedious to comply with the administration attached to each firearm. Before all the liberals start wailing, let me also state that I have never killed anyone, and I don't intend shooting anyone in the foreseeable future. In fact, I have never even so much as raised a hand in anger or been in a fight. *Ergo*, I am not a violent person.

If you are one of those people who, like me, feels that an armed man is a citizen and an unarmed man a subject, maybe you understand this argument already – in which case, go and have a snack or read the next chapter of this book. We probably understand each other. If, however, you work for Gun Free South Africa (GFSA), you'll probably want to shoot me by the end of this piece, which would be an interesting conundrum for you.

Answer yes or no to the following questions to see where you stand:

1 **Do you believe guns kill people?**

2 **Do you believe the government (ie, the police can protect you from bad people who want to kill you?**

3 **Do you think guns are unstable, explosive and go off all the time by accident?**

4 **Do you think you could negotiate with a criminal from behind your**

security gate or alarm system and ask him nicely to leave your house?

5. **Do you believe a can of Mace, a cattle prod, a kitchen knife or your blue belt in karate are effective weapons against a gun-wielding bad guy?**
6. **Do you think, if nobody had guns, criminals would hang up their coats and find real jobs, instead of carrying on with crime and perhaps using a different kind of weapon?**
7. **Do you believe most licensed gun owners shoot to kill instead of shoot to stay alive?**
8. **Do you believe we need more laws and restrictions placed on private, legal gun owners?**

If you answered yes to any of the questions, then you and I are likely to disagree on all of them. We live in a country where it is apparent that ordinary citizens cannot rely on anyone but themselves for their security. Government has made it very difficult for us to own guns because they seek to control us, and only a government that fears its people needs to control them. Wouldn't you rather have a gun and not need it than need a gun and not have it?

Simply put, guns are not the problem, criminals are the problem. It is the desire to do evil, with or without a weapon, that leads to criminal activity. That's why lawyers make such a big deal about intent in criminal matters. Think about it: just because a woman has the equipment to become a prostitute doesn't mean she is one, right? Government and GFSA have no business taking away good people's guns. Leave us alone. By the way, if you need more convincing, or perhaps you crave some backing for the case, think about this: millions of firearm owners in the United States killed nobody yesterday.

Phuza Thursday

As I expect is the situation with you, I have a love/hate relationship with alcohol. The love part is the euphoria and fun and letting down of your hair – the social and wild side of a good drinking experience. The hate is when things go wrong, when stupid things are said and damage is caused – or worse. The hangover isn't even worth crediting; it is the admission by the body that something messy has happened inside you. It's the expensive bus fare back from happy-land.

We have a terrible social problem in South Africa, and much of it stems from our addiction to alcohol. Binge-drinkers, full-blown alcoholics and the people around them all suffer from the nasty side of drinking. I think of myself as neither a teetotaller nor an alcoholic. As with most things, there is a more harmonious middle ground. I have had my share of the truly drunken evenings, and an equal proportion of the sober, sensible kind. I have decided that I will not think of one as superior to the other, but I have made for myself some rules, to keep things manageable.

1 I won't drive after more than one drink

I have done this on many occasions and have mercifully been spared death, once or twice having escaped a car accident with some scrapes, cuts and pains only. I don't need to experience that again. If I'm not sure, I'll get a cab. Seriously. I wish everyone else would do the same (the charity of which I am patron, Headway, looks after people who have come out of such accidents less fortunately than I, with traumatic brain injury).

2 I won't get drunk around people I don't know well

unless there are at least one or two sober people who have my back. Drunk people can be dangerous and instinctive. I have been both the tormented and tormentor in a few such situations, and the regret and patchy memories the next day can turn a good night into a lengthy stretch of paranoia.

3 Know when the party's over

There is nothing worse than a lingering, sad hanger-on who can't let go of the night. Happily I have found fatigue usually takes me instinctively away, earlier than the dregs …

4 Put your phone away for emergency use only

An ex-girlfriend's number in the hands of a drunk can be a highway to hell. You're at the party to be with the people who are *at* the party. People on the phone are not there with you, so don't drag them there digitally.

I have broken every one of my rules, and might stray and do so again in the future. I'm not a self-flagellating, guilt-riddled self-loather, but part of my reason for writing all of this down is that I hope to reinforce the rules in my own head. I have been too lucky in the past – and my luck might not last. Let your brain make the decisions, before taking action. Alcohol isn't dangerous in and of itself; it's what you do with alcohol that can make or break small and very large things.

You're not Gordon fucking Ramsay

People behave very strangely when they eat in public. From the time communal cave-eating began, I'm sure people found reasons to enjoy and become annoyed with each other. Louis XIV used to dine in public, mostly to keep his etiquette-obsessed nobility on their toes with new tricks, but also to teach the ordinary people how to eat properly. My grandparents never let my father and uncle eat with them until they learned respectable table manners. Evidently they only got this right at about age 14. These days, we all get together in each other's homes or at restaurants.

Shelf upon shelf in most respectable bookstores groan under the weight of books about famous restaurants and their food. If you bought this book along with one of those cookbooks, I hope you're ashamed. As for restaurants, there are people whose sole job it is to appraise these places. And yet, there are some things that happen in restaurants that are so peculiar they occur almost nowhere else.

Have you seen, for example, the couples who go to fancy places, order their food and then sit silently, ignoring each other for the duration of the meal? Have you seen the wives who order for their thin little husbands, devour their own meal, and then consume his, too? Fat people have a way, you might have noticed, of pulling their arms up close to them, like a *Tyrannosaurus rex*, whenever there's a lot of food around.

Have you seen those tables of 20 people or more who order a single focaccia and a jug of water and yet stay for a good few hours? I know some restaurant managers who charge them a fee just for taking up space. Quite right.

Then there are those who make excruciatingly fussy orders: 'I'll have the lamb vindaloo, but with noodles instead of rice and in place of the sambals could I have a steak tartare with some sliced banana and avocado? Also, don't make it too hot ... and bring some spirit vinegar on the side.' A menu is not a guideline; it's a *numerus clausus* of options. Just choose something; it's not your kitchen and you're not Gordon fucking Ramsay. While I'm here, it's worth noting that too many people who complain about their order have already put away about half of it when they decide they don't like it and ask for a replacement dish or refund. This is not on. These people are cheapskates and should be double-billed.

Speaking of billing, the tip-thief is a common problem. I used to have a friend who, when the bill arrived, would add only enough to make the total. He'd pay last, and, without tipping, would then disapprovingly mention that we hadn't added a tip and needed to cough up more. He, of course, got away with paying a third of his cost every time. We knew, but were too polite to keep bringing it up. When it comes to splitting the bill, there are some very bizarre customs: some people itemise every entry, calculating to the last cent just how much they're responsible for; others throw in more or less what they think their share is, with a little bit extra for the tip; and others begrudge those who had a slightly more costly meal than they had. All in all, it's a very complex situation.

The restaurants themselves come with their own swathe of irritations: soft drinks made in machines, paper napkins, waiters who either watch you eat or ask you questions while your mouth is full ... And don't think the customer is always king: There is a fine restaurant I know where the chef will not allow you to add any salt or pepper to his meal, and where if you ask for salt he comes out of the kitchen in a fury and tells you to leave.

Sometimes an establishment will have some kind of horrible water feature at its entrance, usually with a huge volume of chlorine in it. This is guaranteed to put you off your meal while it poisons your lungs. Makes the whole place smell like the First World War. I have also never really understood the seafood restaurant that makes sea creatures in an aquarium watch us eat their relatives, as if in some way this might enhance the experience.

A lot of people will ask for a doggy bag if they didn't manage to finish their meal. Ordinarily you'd think how sweet it was of them to consider their hungry German Shepherd at home. The reality is that it's for them to finish at some later date, and their greed won't let them leave even the tiniest of leftovers to be sent back to the kitchen.

With the aforementioned bill comes my own pet hate: the mints. There are some that are perfectly acceptable – actual mints, or those nice butterscotchy sweets. Sometimes, cruelly, you end up with those dreadful chocolate/coffee drop things that spoil a wonderful meal and pollute your palate with a revolting aftertaste.

What we know about going out for dinner is that it can be, at any time, either a life-affirming pleasure or an ordeal. It comes down to who you're with and where you go, and seldom what you eat.

Cows are the perfect machines for turning grass into steak

Let's face it: we human beings are omnivores. There's nothing like a good steak. I find vegetarians and vegans quite disturbing. We have teeth and jaws especially evolved to deal with plant and animal material in our diet. To this point, the best evolutionary argument against herbivorous behaviour among humans is the uselessness of our appendix, or caecum. This purpose of this pathetic and now unnecessary organ was to host certain bacteria that specifically break down cellulose, the main component in plant cell walls. No doubt at some point in the evolution of our species we ate rather a lot of leaves, and so needed this organ quite a lot more, but somewhere between that point and the present we have naturally selected against it. Animals like koala bears have very long appendices for this precise purpose. But we're not koala bears. Therefore the appendix is now an organ that is optional to a long and healthy life.
I have a sickly-looking friend who insists he is a vegan. He is convinced that by eating a few soya beans and some tofu he can absorb enough protein to avoid hurting commercially reared beef cattle and other creatures he supposes have a face and ought to be spared the very purpose for which they have been genetically engineered. This latter term ought not frighten you into the assumption that Dr Moreau had to be called to build a monster from a loping, kindly, long-lashed dairy cow. Over many hundreds of years, we have carefully bred very suitable types of cattle particularly for their mouthwatering meat.

I can never say no to a fine, medium-rare Argentine steak, cooked to perfection and satisfying to a utopian degree, so how on earth do these hippies manage to? The most sensible argument from vegetarians is the one against factory-farmed, artificial-hormone-filled poultry and livestock.

The sad and degraded living conditions of these poor creatures notwithstanding, I can only imagine the resulting produce to be poor in quality. Like most of our supermarket fruit – ever more watery, bland and disappointing – I worry that a cow without enough room, natural fodder and care and attention might end up giving me a bland degustative experience.

Having said that, I still find vegetarians a problem in a social context. It used to be an easy thing to invite a few friends round for a hearty braai. In South Africa, this is almost ritualistic behaviour. Since the advent of these dietary cults, just the extension of an invitation becomes a quagmire of potential pitfalls. A while ago, I suggested dinner to a group of friends. Some didn't eat meat; some ate meat, but only chicken or fish; some ate meat, but wanted it blessed by some religious officer, or insisted that they were informed fully of the manner of their meal's death. It was so difficult just to decide upon an agreeable restaurant. We ended up at a steakhouse.

You will find, if you inspect your mouth in the bathroom mirror, that you are equipped with molars, incisors and canines. Each of these teeth has an important role to play in the first step of the digestive process. If you insist on being a vegan or vegetarian, then I suggest that you have the dentist pluck out your canine teeth. That way, people will know what to expect when you smile at the waiter, and won't be shocked when you order a salad and some broad beans at a steakhouse. No meat? Fine. No meat teeth. Problem solved.

Brain power

Have you ever had a brain fart? That's usually when we remember we even have a brain. What was I saying? Seriously, the brain is home to your mind, your personality, your memories and your hopes for the future. It deserves a bit of recognition.

The brain is by far the most complicated and incredible organ in the human body. You don't need me to tell you that. What is less obvious is the way it all works. We know so little about how neurons fire, the function of the charges carried by sodium and potassium ions along axons and dendrites (as the small fibres that carry the impulses are known – even if they do sound very rude), and how they carry complicated instructions and communications over the synapses at the end of each nerve fibre. OK, I did learn a bit about this in high school, but that's all I know. It isn't just all *I* know; it's pretty much all *we* know.

We know about the grey matter of the cerebrum, cerebellum, medulla oblongata, pons varolii and spinal cord. The grey matter is made up of the actual nerve cell bodies. The other stuff – what they call the white matter – is a huge bundle (like a bunch of cables tied together in your TV room) of fibres that run out in all directions from the cells. When you want to move your arm, a neuron in the brain fires off an instruction down from the grey matter, along the fibre and to a muscle, which responds by flexing to lift the chunk of meat that makes your upper limb. Each fibre is covered in what they call a myelin sheath, which is fancy anatomical terminology for insulation.

The cerebrum is the spongy pink-grey stuff that kids draw when they colour in the brain with crayons. It is folded; the increased surface area, like the hills and valleys you see when you look out of the window of a plane, provide more space for tissue than would a flat, smooth surface. It is here in the frontal cerebrum that we have our higher brain functions. Right behind your forehead and above your eyes is where you do all your complex thinking, where you consider whether something is right or wrong, where you come up with ideas and inventions. It is this part of the brain that we need to decode if we ever hope to know who and what we are in physiological terms. That's the anatomy lesson over.

Do you know anyone who has been in an accident and has been lucky enough to walk away unscathed? Many are not so fortunate. The brain can be injured like any other part of the body, even when there is no obvious external damage. Lives are changed in a split-second.

I am the patron of an inspiring little organisation called Headway-Gauteng. Essentially, it's a non-profit organisation that looks after people who have suffered brain injuries – people who were living a normal productive lives one moment, and through some unfortunate incident sustained head injuries. These could be caused by a car accident, sporting accident, a fall or an assault. It is very difficult to imagine, since we know so little about the brain, just how awful it must be to suffer an injury to this part of your body. But we can see what such an injury might do, and the results can be devastating.

In my first year with Headway, I attended their Christmas party and met a kid. Let's call him Byron. Before I met him, Byron had been a happy, active, quite normal South African boy. He played soccer, rode a bike, did well at school. He could be just like you or your kids at 10 years. But poor Byron ended up in a car accident that was not of his doing, and which he could not have avoided. Byron suffered a horrible head injury that severely impaired his ability to walk, speak, eat, drink, move and express emotion. I shall never, as long as I live, forget the painful, tired and weary look in the eyes of Byron's mother. She looked like she was carrying the weight of the world on her shoulders – and yet she managed a smile. So did his dad and his little sister – who later on diligently helped Byron to eat and drink, as you might help an infant. A lump came to my throat, and it is no exaggeration to say that these people utterly changed my attitude.

I was suddenly embarrassed about all the stupid things I thought were my problems. I felt privileged and spoilt and emotionally shallow. When I think of that day, I still do.

Byron's story has a less depressing second chapter. Every year I see him improve: from a wheelchair to crutches, then to a single crutch, and now an unsteady, but courageously unassisted walk. That's it – courage. That is exactly the word I'd use to describe the whole family. Struck by indescribable tragedy, they – and so many others like them – are the reason I got involved with Headway. The organisation's mostly volunteer staff – family members, occupational therapists, doctors, physiotherapists, kind helpers and expert neurologists – make me feel that I couldn't do enough if I did only what they so wonderfully do. And it all comes down to the brain.

Some people think I'm clever, and some people think I'm stupid. Those two opinions could just as easily come from one person, on a bad day. By and large my brain seems to work, and I am grateful for this faculty. It's something most of us take for granted. If we are just great carcasses of organs, meat, blood and bones, then our brains give that what a who. You are your brain. We'll never know if souls really exist, and it doesn't matter if they do. We know that locked up in that cranium of ours is every facet of our personality, knowledge, emotion, sense and nonsense.

Horsing around

I once had a very beautiful and bubbly girlfriend who said how excited she was to go the 'Durban July in Cape Town'. She's probably is one of many who don't know the difference, but she's also no longer my girlfriend. The fact that she couldn't spell didn't help the prospects for the relationship, either.

Be that as it may, the Met and Durban July are the only horse races everyone in South Africa knows about. That's because they are more like fashion parades in an otherwise much, much more boring sport. It shouldn't really be called a sport, though, because, as with motor racing, the driver or jockey has less to do with it than the car or horse. The only people I can think of who love horse racing are Lebanese bookmakers, widowers and the Queen.

I've been to the July and the Met a few times, and I will say that it's fun if your liver can handle a full day's heavy drinking in the sun, and if you have an appreciation for ladies who wear extraordinary, sometimes sexy and occasionally frightening outfits. For most of the spectators, it's just a day-long party. The vast majority of them wouldn't know if the twelfth was a horse, dog or capybara race. They wouldn't care even If they did know.

And shame, the jockeys. Have you ever met a jockey? They're like squeaky-voiced hobbits who spend their entire diminutive lives losing weight and riding horses that get all the attention when they win. They're also terribly aggressive little people. I have no idea why, but they seem extra thin-skinned and are easily provoked to anger and violence. Many of them have exceptionally pretty girlfriends, and some have lots of money. I'm not saying that the latter begets the former, but I'm not not saying it either.

One of the other things that makes horse racing bearable is the names people give their horses: Hoof-Hearted, Doremifasolatido, Oh No! Its My Mother-In-Law!, Why The Long Face?, Arrrrrr and the ubiquitous Really Fast Horse. If I had a horse, I'd call her Sarah Jessica Parker. I'd like to hear the nasal commentator saying: 'It's Sarah Jessica Parker coming in from the back, pushing hard, just a few furlongs behind Archbishop of Canterbury.' 'Yes, Martin, Sarah Jessica Parker had a problem with her hind leg yesterday, and both her vet and farrier had to be called in to have a look, but it seems they gave her the all clear and just watch her go, out there on the track!' What a prize mare she would be.

The arguments about whether the sport is cruel or not are arguments that, for once, I don't want to get into. I know too little to be informed in any way about the way horses who break their legs are shot and their meat sent off to the lion park. All I know is that it would appear to be a thriving modern attraction, and that Durban and Cape Town can host all the socialites in the land for a day each. The quality of these socialites notwithstanding, if everyone is having fun, it can't be too bad.

Life begins where fundamentalism ends

We're a civilised bunch in South Africa. Well, we like to think so. Abortion is completely legal here, and I for one applaud our government for getting that sorted out. But there are less civilised places in the world – like America!

Last year, a famous abortionist called Dr George Tiller was shot while entering his local church to pray to the God he loved and clearly believed in. The guy who shot him believed in God, too. The abortionist thought he was doing God's work, and so did the shooter. Both of them were stupid. If there is a God, he showed not the slightest bit of interest in either man or his principles. The one is dead and the other going to prison, to be sodomised.

Abortion is a very prickly issue in the USA – way more than in any other modern, first-world country. The 'pro-life', right-wing evangelicals, on the one hand, believe that abortion is just wrong – it's the taking of a human life. They believe that a 'soul' is created with the conception of a zygote and that from this point the life of the ensuing conglomerate of cells is sacred. On the other hand, we have the 'pro-choice' lobby; these people believe that a woman has the right to decide what to do with her body and to decide whether or not she would like to see a pregnancy through. Neither are likely to come to any compromise any time soon.

There are some much dumber arguments, though. Some pro-lifers are willing to concede that if the foetus is the result of a rape, then there are grounds for termination. But that makes no sense at all, since what you're then saying is that life is sacred unless the kid's dad is an arsehole. Sounds a little subjective.

The fact is that abortions will happen, and they may as well happen under the protection of the law and in the safety and security of medical care. Any doctor who assists women with abortions does not only what is good for the patient, but also what is good for our species. There are already far too many unwanted, abandoned and orphaned 'sacred little souls' left to fend for themselves on this planet.

Excellent or average?

Grammy Award-winning Lebo M, the genius behind *The Lion King*, was our guest on 5FM one morning. He said something that puzzled me at first, and then I began to think it was terribly clever and quite true. He said that we South Africans are very hard on ourselves.

He's right. We are loath to congratulate ourselves when we do well and quick to criticise ourselves when we don't. Think about it: when we win the Rugby World Cup, we celebrate for a few days at most. When we lose a cricket Test match, we bitch and complain and degrade ourselves for weeks. It's all very masochistic. I think we don't believe, as a nation, that we're entitled to do well. Why do you think that is?

In 2010, South Africa hosted the FIFA World Cup. For the years leading up to this most prestigious sporting event in the world, South Africans of all colours bemoaned the fact that we would never be ready, the stadia were behind schedule, the Gautrain would be a disaster and our transport system wouldn't cope, our team was useless and that, in every likelihood, Australia would end up hosting the tournament. Not only was it one of the best World Cup events ever, it integrated the country in a way nobody could have imagined. For a short while, we were all just South Africans united in our pride as the world's cameras documented the proceedings. Not one month later, it all came crashing down with the health and education strikes, which smashed our national joy to smithereens.

Every year on *Idols*, I hear the same bleating about how we're not as good as *American Idol*. Sometimes I even catch myself thinking that, too. We certainly don't have the population, the chutzpah that is instilled in Americans from birth, or the mega-production budgets. When a South African artist goes overseas to sing or act or dance, we assume it's because they couldn't make it here, and they aren't likely to make it there either. They can't win. We can never just say, 'Well done!' When a South African who has done well passes us in the street, or we see them on TV, we make snide remarks, never building them or the nation up, but rather tearing them down. It boils down to insecurity, and I've heard and seen this strange self-flagellation in even my most intelligent and confident friends. I think psychologists call it projection.

A South African will never say, 'Damn! I'm good!', even when he or she is. Americans, Australians, even Nigerians, have no problem admitting that they're amazing, especially, but not limited to, when they win. The fact is, we're not the best at everything, but we're not as bad as you may think.

What is even more alarming is that we're so quick to settle for a mediocre status quo. We accept sluggish service and still reward it with a tip. We accept deadlines being missed, and we are quick to make excuses or play the blame game for not achieving excellence. We blame apartheid, government, the boss, the staff, BEE, not enough time, not enough money or not enough support. You can add your own personal blame barrier to the list.

It's about time that we stop this prolonged throat-clearing, start refusing mediocrity and begin demanding excellence. We don't make excuses when we succeed. Why should we accept them not to succeed?

With our stories, people, talent and history, we should stop being so negative and average, and when a fellow countryman is above average we should celebrate them. Stop yourself next time you're about to tear down a local who has the talent or balls to stick their head out above the crowd; remember it's actually you who's being average in doing so.

Pastor Paparazzi

The Advertising Standards Authority (ASA) this year banned a Nigerian evangelist in Durban, who claims he's a pastor, from further claiming that he can cure, among other things, AIDS, cancer, blindness and quadriplegia. It is the first good thing I have seen the ASA do, and I wish to praise them for it.

Don't you agree that taking advantage of the sick, the stupid, the bereaved, the emotionally vulnerable and the gullible is despicable? Today, there are powerful new ways of exploiting the simpering masses by promising them much and delivering paltry stage magic, usually to gasps and howls from the crowd who wish-think it to be true. Since the advent of television, evangelical Christians have achieved rock-star status and have been dealing out 'miracle cures' and 'faith healing' to ever-wider audiences.

What I find fascinating is the celebrity status afforded to so many charismatic pastors. Beyond healing, materialism has found a prominent place in their teachings; if you donate your hard-earned cash to the church, it will make you rich, or book you a place in heaven.

I have often been criticised for daring to question religion or religious leaders. Religious scandals have been well documented for centuries from the medieval inquisitions to the Jimmy Swaggarts of today. You barely have to lift your head up before you're confronted with some ugly story. Do you remember Jimmy Swaggart?

In 1988, he was implicated in a sex scandal involving a prostitute that resulted in his being defrocked, and do you think he didn't go out and do it again? There seem to be countless charlatans of the cloth who enjoy millionaire lifestyles that involve sex, corruption and fraud. It's just like politics or big business. Sometimes it's both of those two.

South Africa has also had its fair share of high-profile pastor scandals. Perhaps the best known, and the source of much gossip with his colourful rags-to-riches story, is Pastor Ray. Ray McCauley went from being a nightclub bouncer to winner of the Mr South Africa title in the 1970s to becoming the flamboyant founder of the Rhema Bible Church. Pastor Ray has received a great deal of media attention not only for his lavish lifestyle, divorce scandals and health and financial woes, but also for Rhema's lavish 30th birthday party last year. It was a paparrazzo's dream. The guests were glittering A-listers, including politicians, executives, actors, singers, sporting stars and, not least, MaNtuli, President Zuma's most spendthrift wife.

Pastor Ray's style, like that of so many larger-than-life religious figures, is characterised by celebrity, bling and the way he convinces people to give their hard-earned money to the church in order to become even richer. He wears shiny suits, works the stage, and attracts thousands of faithful followers. Even President Zuma himself paid a strategic visit to Rhema and Pastor Ray when he was on the campaign trail. There is influence indeed in being shepherd to the flock.

Religion is an important part of many people's lives, and some will prefer to turn a blind eye to these shameful shenanigans. Some will argue that taking advantage of the willing or ignorant is perfectly acceptable business, like when a casino promises you a jackpot and you lose your life savings. I'm afraid I can't agree. Business is a fair exchange of one thing for another. If you're selling *x* and I'm prepared to pay *y*, we are doing business. If you ask for too much, I can decline the offer, and you can similarly decline mine if you think it too low. What is too low is to promise *x* and deliver nothing, to lie to vulnerable people and take advantage of their sad circumstances.

Paparazzi pastors are inevitably gifted storytellers, and sometimes talented performers, but I wonder how sustainable it is for any business to rely on one person's gift of the gab and ability to pull a crowd by promising personal enrichment, wealth and miracle cures. Don't you? Being a religious leader does not make that person any more moral than it makes an atheist amoral.

'Lord, Grant me the serenity to accept the things I cannot change, the courage to change the things I cannot accept, and the wisdom to hide the bodies of those people I had to kill today because they pissed me off.' Amen.

Karatara

A friend in Knysna once told me of a place ... She told me on a stormy night, while the sea smashed against the rocky outcrops of the Knysna Heads, while small boats tied to the pier tried to hold on, ropes pulled taut to their moorings, while the wind howled and the skies grew dark outside. She looked around to make sure nobody was listening and then began to whisper the story of a hidden secret, a place called Karatara.

If you ever read Dalene Matthee's superb novel, *Kringe in 'n Bos* (Circles in the Forest), you'll know all about the *bosmense* of the forests. Rough, violent, self-sufficient and fiercely independent people, many of them spent years in the isolated wilderness, some never able to read, write or speak intelligibly. They made a very modest living by cutting wood. In 1939, the South African government removed all woodcutters from the forests surrounding Knysna and gave them government pensions. They also relocated most of them to Karatara. This was where my friend's story began.

Karatara is now a desperately poor and miserable township peopled by the descendants of woodcutters. She explained that the people were disconnected from the modern world (there is only one road in or out of the little town), unused to amenities like electricity, running water and sewerage systems, and insular and often inbred. She described men, women and children of the kind you see in movies about hicks from the Appalachians, the kind that civilisation left behind. All of this in 2011, in South Africa, on the Garden Route.

I don't find monster movies scary; I find horror movies featuring human monsters scary. You know, the ones where some community irradiated by illegal nuclear tests many decades ago has become a rampaging band of terrifying mutants? The ones where whole families exist by hunting other humans, keeping their young in cages or tied to the front porch, and where the girls give birth to incestuous offspring in their early teens. I'm not saying this is what happens in places like the one my friend described, but that's where my imagination took me. I pictured broken-down cars and rusty fence-poles marking the edge of town that no civilised people cross, signs scrawled in blood warning outsiders to keep out – but where the letter k in 'keep' faces the other way. I shivered at the thought that these people would head out into the forests at night, armed with edged weapons and howling at the moon, to hunt for food.

'I'm sure it's not like that ...' I wondered aloud, interrupting her. 'Is it like that?' She looked confused, and I realised she had been talking about something else while I painted pictures in my head.

Now I don't know about you, but this sort of place fascinates me. It's amazing because it is the result of social engineering. It's amazing because just down the road from you and I might be a community of people who have neither heard of the internet nor used a toothbrush. It's also the sort of place most people seem embarrassed to talk about, maybe because most of the poor people there are white, or maybe because they're so backward. All I know I heard from that friend of mine ... and now I'm fascinated, and a little scared. Even the name Karatara is a bit creepy.

Getting the house in order

I've never imagined for a second that I was perfect. I know I'm full of stupidity, occasional myopia and some prejudice, but that doesn't mean I'm not capable of correcting myself. I thought 2011 might be a good time to clear the air. To those I have offended, here is your long-awaited apology:

To former President Mbeki: I'm sorry I compared you to Stalin and begged the ANC to unseat you in Polokwane. You were a thinker and you were sensitive, like the poets of old. I was a loud white guy who criticised you a lot, and it annoyed you and made you justifiably petulant. I'll bring you a bottle of whisky in Killarney if you will let me in at the gate and not set your dogs, or Essop Pahad, on me. Even Julius Malema says you deserve some credit now. Hindsight can be pretty useful, sir.

To Cindy Nell: I'm sorry I said that you didn't really win Miss South Africa, and that Sami Sabiti read the results the wrong way round. You're a beautiful woman and you turn me on. It must have been my inability to charm you that frustrated me into being nasty. When I'm emotional, I say stupid things. Let's have a pool party.

To the late Minister Manto Tshabalala-Msimang: I'm not glad you're dead. That's a hateful, hurtful, vicious thing to say, and I only wanted you out of the Cabinet, not out of living altogether. If only I had become an atheist sooner, then God would have ignored my evil prayers, instead of taking you away. I deserve some shame. If you were here right now, I'd buy some few rounds to try to make up. Jack Daniel's, right?

To Comrade Blade Nzimande: you're not ugly, Blade. What I said was ugly, and it turned me a little uglier. Watch this season of *Idols* and you'll see how much I have deteriorated. Bad things happen because I deserve them.

To Helen Zille: I'm sorry about all the horrible jokes (concubines, Botox, etc), bad impersonations and on-air questions about toilets. You work really hard, and you deserve more respect than I have given you. You're also looking really good, and you have much to be proud of, even if your pantsuits aren't as nice as Hillary Clinton's.

To Damon Kalvari, Thabo Modisane's assistant: you're not really so bad – just a bit odd. But you still have to work from the back room for your own protection.

To Alec Erwin, former Minister of Public Enterprises: your hair looks great!

To all the failed *Idols* contestants: I might have been crass and insensitive, especially in the first season or two. The show is not about me, it's about you – and I've finally grown up and realised that. Randall, I admit, is unlikely to have the same epiphany, but I can man up and apologise.

To everyone else who may have tuned in to my radio show, seen me on TV or read a tweet, post or blog, and found something revolting in my delivery or content, I thought I'd better own the bad.

Odd man out

Sticky floors, dusty surfaces, curling carpets: I can't concentrate. A painting hanging at an awkward angle: I'm sorry, I stopped listening to you. The bookshelf with a few haphazard books placed horizontally on top of the others: I'm starting to fixate.

I grew up tidying up my immediate surroundings instinctively, and because it made me happy, not because I was ever scolded or admonished for having an untidy room. In fact, my mother thought it was a stroke of luck that she never needed to pick up after me. When I was a small child, I'm sure there was no such thing as obsessive-compulsive personality disorder (OCPD).

Years later, when I went with a friend (who also happened to be a third-year Psychology major) to see Jack Nicholson in *As Good as it Gets*, I found it uncomfortable that everyone was laughing at the rituals and eccentricities of Jack's character. I knew why he was doing those things. The rest of the cinema found it laughable. After the movie, my psychologist friend helpfully pointed out that I only ever crossed a threshold with my right foot, that I counted things that it was not necessary to count, and that I found it impossible to concentrate if something in my environment was out of place. According to her, I had a mild kind of OCPD.

Growing up in my family, it was unnecessary to seek the advice of therapists, shrinks and people who deal with all kinds of mental illness. We have a few mad uncles and aunts (properly mad, mind you, not like the wacky ones most families say they have – one of them is, as we speak, growing vegetables for aliens in his one-acre garden), but we don't have a very high regard for the softer kinds of anxiety or depression. Certainly my 'neatness', as they referred to it, was nothing to be concerned about. And so I maintain that it isn't. Had I told my father I had OCPD or ADHD, he would have given me a wallop. In the end, I turned out mostly alright.

My only challenge is to focus, to concentrate on what I'm being told, to maintain a level of engaged conversation, when a crooked doorway, funny smell or untidy tabletop call to me from across the room. They magnetically, forcibly, draw me to correct them, to take notice. I'm not present; I'm straightening the frame, cleaning the TV surface, balancing the vases on the mantelpiece. I drift in and out of the discussion, pretending to pay attention out of politeness. It can be uncomfortable, but I try not to be rude.

There is no way to make sense of this. The only way I can explain it to someone who has no idea of how it works in my head is to make them imagine a house full of clocks, all set to random and different times. Until all those clocks have been set to the right time, there is no way to settle down. To sort these things out, to arrange my life in an organised, clean way, brings me equilibrium. Everything has its place and there must be a place for everything. I don't know why I enter a room with my right foot every time, only that I subconsciously count the steps to make it so. I don't count like Rain Man when I do it. I check locks repeatedly, mostly because I worry that I might not have done it right. Only very rarely does this make me late.

The problem with modern psychology is that we're diagnosing new conditions every few days. People who would have been thought just a little eccentric some years ago are now on a daily regime of medication, or seeing a therapist four times a month. Everyone is on antidepressants; all the kids have ADHD. People are now so self-absorbed that they tell the doctor what they think they need, and will go to any length to avoid even a small amount of strain, stress or difficulty without complaining of a commensurate mental ailment. Parents try to have their children's bad behaviour blamed on some emotional or psychological condition rather than accept that they're bad parents. Poor Johnny can't learn his arithmetic because his brain needs more potassium than other children's do. Little Johnny is so clever he can convince his unstable mother of the same, so she ends up doing his homework for him.

Most of this nonsense isn't a disorder; it's attention-seeking. People watch Dr Phil and listen to radio programmes where experts provide them with excuses to behave badly, antisocially or selfishly. Get over yourself; you're not that special. If Rwandan child soldiers can settle down and get on with their lives by taking a job at the local supermarket, you can stop being depressed, sunshine.

I have relatives who used to keep leopards as pets, who would cut off the sleeves of their jackets if they got too hot, and who would shoot at aircraft if they flew too noisily over the house. At my brother's 21st birthday party, after some rousing speeches, a few of the men insisted on drinking Champagne from their dress shoes. I have signs in my guest bathrooms that forbid poo-ing. My mother thinks the word 'toilet' is much worse than 'motherfucker'. My grandmother made all her guests play a game of general knowledge before they'd be allowed to join her for dinner. A psychologist would have a field day with us. It is because we think we're alright that we're alright. Mental health is within your reach.

Abbottabad Day, not a bad day

No matter how much you hate America (and I certainly don't, but a great many disappointed people do), you have to congratulate them on finding and killing Osama bin Laden.

We're not talking in morally relativistic terms about this man. No freedom fighter was he who claimed unhesitatingly that he had masterminded the killing of thousands of multinational civilians, women and children, on 11 September 2001. No great anti-hero of the poor was this son of a wealthy Saudi construction tycoon, nor an example of the best of Islam, nor a man welcomed by any country except the now-defunct Taliban-run Afghanistan. In short, Osama bin Laden was an enemy of civilisation. Though there may be many areas where a subjective point of view is a matter of debate, in this case there is no wiggle room for opposition. Anyone who can declare that they think Osama bin Laden alive is better than Osama bin Laden dead is declaring themselves an equal enemy of civilisation. Now, I'm not sure about you, but I don't like to allow too much political correctness around discussions to do with my enemies.

I find it telling that there are pockets of people who still like to say 'supposed 9/11 mastermind', since these people obviously conveniently forget, or are ignorant of, Bin Laden's admission of responsibility for, and delight in, those events. I think it equally revealing that those who dislike America conflate this fact with al-Qaeda being anything but a terror organisation. The two are separate matters, and suggest an inability to logically compare apples with apples. These people must be considered dangerous, if only for their lack of reason. The other nutcases we encounter when broaching the topic of Bin Laden are the ones who claim that his assassination was a hoax cooked up by the Obama administration. These conspiracy theories are uttered by the same people who, ten years ago, said that Bush and his government brought down the World Trade Center with controlled explosions. So what they're saying now is that the government didn't kill the guy who didn't bring about 9/11. Very sensible. Get your batshit right, ladies and gentlemen. I suppose it is true that people prefer a conspiracy theory to no theory at all.

The Bin Laden operation in Abbottabad brings something else to mind: that clearly there are places where the most horrible people can live with relative impunity, for at least a few years, sheltered by the communities among whom they hide. The US military made much of their efforts to protect civilians from harm in the raid that led to the death of Bin Laden. In the end there were no civilian casualties. I would not have been so merciful. Doubtless, there were people in that community who aided and abetted Bin Laden and his henchmen. They should be willing to bear their share of the violence that will inevitably follow, as should the nation of Pakistan. Certainly Pakistan should be divested of the substantial foreign aid payments America and Britain have been making to it in return, supposedly, for Pakistani assistance in fighting terror. They have betrayed that charge a little too obviously.

That it took ten years for the world's most powerful nation to hunt down a solitary man is less of an achievement. While his death is a great relief, much devastation, bloodletting and pain has preceded it. I think the US deserves a great deal of applause for destroying this poisonous monster. A respectful, Islamic funeral was apparently given him before they tossed his bullet-riddled corpse into the Arabian Sea. I don't see why it was necessary for someone who did so much harm to the relations between Islam and the rest of the world to be afforded such treatment.

As for Mr bin Laden's obituary, let me be brief and not waste your time:

Osama bin Laden
1957–2011
Punt

Not to be is not the same as to be

If I were to ask you if you believed the sun orbited the earth, if you could turn stone into gold or if you believed in horoscopes and you said no, you wouldn't be taking a position in an equivocal, balanced debate – you'd just be considered sensible. Just as there is no such thing as a non-astrologer, earth-sun geocentrist or an alchemist, it doesn't really mean anything to be an atheist. That is why I object to being asked to fill in anything under 'religion' in surveys and official forms. Saying you're an atheist is not a position; it is an unwillingness to take a conceivably irrational position.

I often find myself in arguments where someone invariably asks how I can believe in nothing. The answer is that I don't believe in nothing … I only know that I don't believe in what they believe in. For most, this seems to be too much, and they usually leave me alone after a promise to pray for my poor soul.

For those who ask what religion I belong to, my answer gives rise to expressions of shock and sometimes pity, unwittingly expressing disbelief. Some assume I must have had some unpleasant experience with a pederastic clergyman, been indoctrinated by a nefarious sect, embraced a wanton and licentious lifestyle, or think I'm being clever. They could save themselves much time and trouble: the truth is, by making a careful study of religion and critically evaluating the veracity of it, I have come to the reasonable conclusion that religion cannot reasonably be right, or very good for us. 'So …,' they say, 'you're an atheist!'

The reaction to this non-controversial conclusion can take one of three forms. The first is violent intolerance, which may end in the zealot murdering me. You laugh now, but let us remember that this is how religious authorities, especially while they were powerful, have treated thinkers and sceptics for many thousands of years. Some of them still do. Heresy, blasphemy and a lack of respect for religion are considered serious offences by very many, even today. This is especially the case in theocracies, where the religion is enmeshed into the socio-political framework.

The second position is that of the person who attempts an argument, insisting that their religion is true, that there is proof and that, among other quite obvious things, they possess old scrolls that prove they're right. Since the same people aren't likely to be proficient in literary criticism or see material evidence as distinct from mythology, the argument cannot go very far. Once all logic runs out (which doesn't take very long in most cases) they find themselves falling back on the position of the third group.

The third reaction to the challenge of atheism is the most thoughtful one. In this group are many intelligent, otherwise quite sensible people who also like to believe in the holy books, religious traditions, spiritual dimensions and other inexplicable phenomena. They'll tell you it isn't important whether Jesus was born of a virgin, whether Abraham actually lived for 175 years or if Muhammad really did ascend into heaven on his winged horse Borak, but they appreciate the more comprehensive, spiritual message. In other words, facts don't matter and nothing is necessarily literal, but the way you feel about it is. An argument can never proceed under these circumstances, just as the claim of a miracle can never be proven under laboratory conditions. Isn't that a cop-out? Either that or it's scriptural cherry-picking. If the latter, they must at least admit they're making their god in their own image and not the other way round.

Your personal experiences and delusions may be very real and meaningful to you, but that does not mean that they are true. If we are to be serious people, and have enough self-respect and respect for the discourse, we cannot address material and important matters by making them subjective. If you heard the voice of an angel, or saw an apparition, or were overcome with emotion during prayer; it might just as well have been a mental disorder, acid flashback or an illusory manifestation of wishful thinking. The cause is not important; your experience does not alter the physical reality. Taxed too far by their duplicitous position, these people most often close with the following profundity: 'It is not about truth or fact or science. It is true to me, I believe it.' 'If that's good enough for you …,' I usually reply, letting them finish the sentence on their own.

By 2012, we should be nearing a point where, thanks to the microscope, the telescope, the computer and the internet, certain facts are established among all but the lunatic fringes, and where humanity can begin to discover new explanations without always being dragged back into redundant argument by those who believe in magic, fairies and spirits. Well, we hope so. The reality is, I'm afraid, much less expansive. Every day, the priests, rabbis and imams put themselves in the awkward position of trying to square an ever-evolving circle. As Christopher Hitchens puts it in *God Is Not Great*:

> Religion has run out of justifications. Where once it used to be able, by its total command of a world-view, to prevent the emergence of rivals, it can now only impede or retard the measurable advances we have made. Sometimes, true, it will artfully concede them. But this is to offer itself the choice between irrelevance and obstruction, impotence or outright reaction, and, given this choice, it is programmed to select the worse of the two.

Stem cell research, family planning, sexual liberation, the pursuit of philosophy and art for their own sake, gender equality, abortion, gay rights, divorce, free speech and even peace – all these things have been, and continue to be, impeded and threatened by the religious-minded and their leaders, and this is unlikely to change. Were I given the power to obliterate religion, I would not. What I would insist upon is that religion and its followers refrain from retarding the advance of human knowledge, that they do not become involved in things they cannot comprehend with the full armoury of their old books and tall hats and smoky offerings.

If you can stomach the irony, see Corinthians 1:13: 'When I was a child, I spake as a child, I understood as a child, I thought as a child: but when I became a man, I put away childish things.' It is time, finally, to honour this rare piece of sensible Scripture and grow up.

Dearly departed

Do you remember all the tortured mourning and emotional flip-flopping that happened when Hansie Cronje's plane crashed into that mountain, back in 2002? I remember people who had never watched a cricket match wailing about how we'd lost a national hero. Perhaps you recall the months before his death, when he embarrassed the whole country and himself by claiming the devil made him take bribes, rig cricket matches and lie to his own wife about, among other things, a horrible leather jacket. Within moments of his death, many people decided he needed to be remembered as a hero. I take exception to this casuistry.

If someone behaves very badly in life, like Osama bin Laden, Pol Pot, Adolf Hitler or Josef Stalin did, death does not absolve them of their lifetime's evils. They don't magically become socially acceptable once they're put in the ground. Of course nobody thinks anything Hansie did could compare with anything an ethnic cleanser might do, but the principle remains: death may be a welcome relief for the dead themselves, and an end to the associated humiliation for their families, but it does not require of me, or of anyone else, a sudden and profound change of attitude towards that person. In simpler terms, becoming dead is not an activity that increases your respectability or places on any of us a duty to be respectful.

This philosophy seems callous and unkind to some critics, and has probably caused me more trouble than almost anything else I have said. I suppose that is because people are afraid of death and because fear cows them. Among the criticisms laid at my door for 'unkind' things I have said about the departed are:

1. **How would you feel if it happened to you? (Usually followed by many exclamation marks!!!)**

2 Just you wait till this happens to your mother or father! (Usually followed by the words 'prick', 'wanker', 'arsehole', or any of those preceded by 'insensitive'.)

3 Imagine how your comments must hurt their family (which is, in some way, the opposite of the previous protestation).

4 You can't joke about death.

5 When someone dies, you cannot speak ill of them (often included is the 'in my culture we honour the dead' rebuke).

6 I hope you burn in hell, you sonofabitch!

Let's deal with each of these on their merits:

1 How would I feel if it happened to me?

Well, I wouldn't feel it. I'd be dead. When you're dead you can't feel anything. Would you like a mint?

2 I should wait until it happens to my mother or father

Well, someone who says this can only be at least as full of malice as they accuse me of being. What they're really saying is: 'I hope this happens to your mother or father so you can feel that pain!' To wish someone dead is, surely, nastier than to talk about him or her in any way after death. Am I wrong about this? I believe this would put the one asking the question on less than stable, and certainly lower, moral ground.

3 Imagine how my comments might hurt the family of the dead

This point has merit. Of course it is unlikely that I mean any harm to the deceased's wife, husband or children, and I might not even know them. For example, Hansie's wife seemed a perfectly amiable and friendly woman when I saw her get married on TV again some time after the crash. My opinion of Hansie was that which anyone might have of a public person; I don't expect her to care about my opinion, let alone be offended by it. If I met her, the very best I could do is be decent enough to tell her that I'm sorry for her pain. To pretend I liked her former husband would be openly deceitful on my part. Sycophantic praise of the dead, as in the case of Dr Manto Tshabalala-Msimang is the kind of revisionist history only practised by the most wicked of politicians and spin doctors. When it comes to family and friends, diplomacy and tact must be used in measured quantities for good manners and to avoid pain, but they cannot mitigate truth. This is why I apologised to the *family* of the former Health Minister, but did not recant the things I said about her. It is a subtle but important distinction.

4 I can't joke about death

Rubbish. You can joke about everything. Anyone who proscribes humour for the rest of us has no sense of it. If something isn't funny, then it isn't funny to you. That is all. Someone else might think it hilarious: just look at the Germans and Scandinavians; they have barely any sense of humour, but will laugh uproariously if someone says 'unterhosen'. What is offensive to you may make someone else's day. It bears repeating that nobody can give you offence; offence is something taken. Don't tell me what I can and can't laugh at. This is 2011, and I do not choose to live in sombre North Korea.

5 I may not speak ill of the dead

Actually, you may speak of the dead in any way you like. Under law the dead have no rights to reputation, dignity or property. So yes, I can speak ill of the dead all day long if I want to. Of course it would probably be in bad taste, but there's no accounting for that, and you certainly can't sue me for it. If your culture has a special reverence for those in the afterlife, then pray to them and they will punish me, but you are not allowed to complain on their behalf. I'll take my chances fighting off spirits and ghosts, and you spend some time thinking about living. If you're right, then I encourage you to speak ill of me when I'm gone and I'll throw pots at you like the poltergeist. Deal?

6 I hope you burn in hell, you sonofabitch! ...

And if there isn't a hell, I can only hope you remain as delightful as you are in life. Honesty is the best policy.

When people get very sick, or when they die, other people begin to treat them differently. Not only is this condescending with regard to the subject, but it makes the person doing it seem less than serious. It tells us a lot about you if you suddenly become friendly and kind to someone in distress but otherwise treat people badly. I think people do this because of how it makes them feel, not because they care about the other person. In some cold part of the reptilian brain, they like it when they're OK and others are not. It's the only time they don't mind being nice, and they get annoyed when I don't fall for the ruse.

By the way, don't you think it was touching how Amy Winehouse's fans formed a line outside her house after she died? A line is what she would have wanted.

Rest in peace, with the condition that you don't bother, and aren't bothered with, the living.

The F-word

Diane Keaton used the F-word on *Good Morning America* a while ago and sent all the viewers hurtling straight down to hell. Did you know swearing can curve your spine, sour the milk in your fridge and invite all kinds of punishment upon you for all eternity? Well apparently the execs at ABC, the network that broadcasts *Good Morning America*, were made to apologise profusely – over and over again, because people were so furious. Parents protested outside their offices, old ladies threatened to embargo the network, and a lot of balding men in office buildings lost hair they didn't even know they had.

That's how powerful profanity is.

Do you think swearing is still a big deal? Before you answer that, please don't bring up the children. Children swear at each other in ways adults can't even fathom. Most of the nasty racial epithets, novel derogatory terminology and just about all the bigoted words come straight off the playground – so let's stop bullshitting ourselves that it's all about protecting the children. Right. Now that's done, what about the rest of us?

If I were to use four-letter words in conversation with you – not swear *at* you, but talk about things and pepper the odd sentence with one or two off-colour words – would you get upset?

David Cameron, the British prime minister, went on a radio show and used the term 'pissed off' and said jokingly that too much twittering could 'make a twat'. Apparently, he also did something very profane. By way of explanation, the word 'twat' refers to the most intimate of feminine areas; it's not a word many South Africans use, but it's not as meek as 'pussy' or as vulgar as 'cunt'.

Now you see, a lot of people might have been enjoying this book up to that last word in the last sentence. It's amazing how powerful some words still are. That C-word is the hydrogen bomb of the common vocabulary. It can prematurely age you. It clangs to the floor in conversation like someone dropping a tray of crystal glasses. It's the word of which certain respectable women would say: 'Now I don't mind piss and shit, but that C-word I will not tolerate ...' In short, there is no word that can cause more offence, and yet I find myself asking: why that is so? Who knows what we're trying to protect by banishing the dirty words, but we're told they're bad and rude and shouldn't be allowed.

I happen to have grown up in a house where my very respectable parents both swore. Often the only appropriate word was a swearword (even the term 'swearword' sounds like it was made up in a kindergarten). Watching the rugby with my father unleashed a panoply of foul and disgusting language that I regard as some achievement in passion. As a result of this sort of thing, I don't really take much notice of other people's swearing, and I try to keep mine in check only among people I don't know terribly well or don't want to. The old excuse that swearing belies a lack of vocabulary can't be true for me because I think I use rather a lot of other words, too.

I had a girlfriend who would wince every time I used foul language. She would berate me every time I did it. She told me it offended her and was disrespectful. She is no longer my girlfriend, but not for that reason – although it did bother me that something so childish should be important to her. Like with most things, it's all in the tone, and the eye, of the beholder.

Diane Keaton may be irritating for any number of reasons (she dresses like a man, for example), but she's not dangerous, and neither is the word 'fuck'. The only reason that word is still shocking in some places is because of the grannies who protest when it's used. Either you're one of those people who swear or you aren't, but surely it doesn't matter?

There is such a thing as too much and too coarse a variety of swearing, usually aboard ships, in diesel mechanics' workshops and in Johannesburg. The people involved use swearwords because they don't have any others. They make the case harder to defend for those of us who make careful use of swearing. I'd think nothing less of a smart, interesting or sexy person dropping in a 'fuck' here or a 'piss' there, but the same doesn't apply to a foul-mouthed drunk in a bar.

Do you go cold when Ozzy Osbourne mouths off? Not likely. He has opted to make swearwords his usual discourse. Of course, it becomes funny again if you put him at a table with a priest, but it's funny, not impactful. What am I getting at? If swearing still bugs you, that's really your business. You're like those Victorian ladies who never acknowledged sex. You're quaint ... Thank you for being so quaint; now you can fuck off.

Do unto others

There shouldn't have to be an excuse. We shouldn't do it because we like Madiba or because other people are doing it, too. We shouldn't need national campaigns on the radio to galvanise us into action. We should just do it. Paying our taxes, voting and watching the news aren't our only civic responsibilities – but some people think they are. I met a guy last week who said he was doing nothing for the country because 'The government aren't doing nothing for me.' His attitude and grammar were both very wrong.

Countries don't work or fall apart only because of governments – and ours is no exception. Businesses, NGOs, concerned individuals and small clubs and groups can have just as much, and sometimes more, effect than the machinery of state. People who sit and wait for governments to do things for them wait for a long time, usually forever.

I don't know about you, but I'm sick of people who sit back and moan about how government must build them a house, educate their children, look after their health. Those who imagine government to be a machine that magically puts out services without anything being put in are ignorant indeed. The problem is that the non-contributors in our economy are increasing by proportion faster than any other group – and they're costing us more and more every year. It simply isn't sustainable.

There are three types of adult human beings on earth. We're mostly required to be self-sufficient. If you are not, you're in the bottom third – and in the way. These are the lazy, tired, apathetic people who long ago forgot the basic principles of survival and need everyone else's help to make a living. They can't get a job, make a job or even think about a job. Some have a valid excuse, but most are merely living organisms. They perform only the functions that an amoeba performs: they eat, sleep, procreate, defecate and die.

Those who are self-sufficient are the next third. These people live, but their generosity ends there. They don't add to the world, except for themselves. They're just a little less parasitic than the former group, and you'll know them by the way they tell you how hard they work. I know some people who make lots of money and live very exciting lives but put nothing back in. I know that they have never helped anyone other than themselves.

The final third is the group that changes the world for the better. These are the people who not only look after themselves, but also manage to lend a hand to other people – donating their money, time, care or expertise to add value wherever they go. They fund philanthropic projects, attend public forums, help out at a charity, plant trees, put up statues and write to Parliament. They help their employees, donate money to worthy causes and pick up litter.

When you consider the impact a man such as Nelson Mandela has had on the human race, consider your own place. Which of the three groups do you fit into?

Little people are big right now

Don't you find midgets fascinating? My favourite character on *Boston Legal*, Bethany Horowitz, is a little person. She's aggressive and overly sensitive, but I like her. I really like midgets. I like having them at parties, for example, but they cost a fortune! Did you know that hiring a midget or dwarf to serve drinks will cost you about R1 700 an hour, per dwarf. Outrageous …

Here's another thing I learned last week: 'midget' is an offensive term. You're apparently not meant to use it. Midgets don't like it. I looked it up on the internet and discovered that, in the first half of the 20th century, 'midget' was a medical term that referred to an extremely short but normally proportioned person, and was used in contrast to 'dwarf', which denoted disproportionate shortness.

So, in other words, there are two different kinds of little people – dwarves and midgets. This is startling. I didn't know. Did you? In future, I will correct people who get it wrong, and maybe the little people will thank me with a smile or a nod of the head. An exciting new world of dwarves and midgets awaits me. It's probably not very PC, but little people *are* interesting, and it's probably very patronising and deeply offensive, but I can't help looking at them. At a party recently, I met a midget and immediately asked her if she was doing OK in the crowd. She responded that it was quite claustrophobic (as you'd imagine crotch level in a crowd might be). I asked her if she'd like to go up on my shoulders instead, and she was affirmative. I obliged. She spent about ten minutes on my shoulders. It was fun for both of us, but I did get disparaging looks from a few people. I can only assume they were jealous that they didn't have a midget of their own.

Little people have come a long way. Less than forty years ago, they could only get work in circuses and freak shows. Now they're able to do almost any job they like and drive cars. They have families (some with normal-sized children), and it won't be long before we have a dwarf in Parliament. Viva the little people, viva!

9/11 – 10 years on

2011 is the ten-year anniversary of 9/11, the day America changed. All those years ago this really had an impact on me, as it did on so many of us. Looking back, this is something that hasn't changed for me and something I still really care about.

On 11 September 2001 the world you woke up to was a different place. Your grandchildren and great-grandchildren will one day ask you what you were doing when the World Trade Center came down. It's amazing to think that America, the most powerful nation on earth, the guardian of democracy and the leader of the free world, had fallen prey to an attack on US soil that amounted to, in the words of President George W Bush, a national tragedy. America lost her innocence. New York City had its back broken, because if they can break it there, they'll break it anywhere.

Exactly a year before 9/11, I flew into New York City for the first time. When you land in New York, imagine seeing immediately to your left, over the water, quite possibly the most recognisable skyline in the world. In the centre, an island, packed full of the tallest buildings you've ever seen. In the early-morning light of my arrival in New York, some of the buildings were glittering in the reflected sun. You would recognise the spires, towers and domes of many of the grandest buildings in the world, but above all you know it's New York because of the highest buildings in the city, the twin Trade Towers that rose up at the toe of Manhattan Island. I remember seeing the towers guarding the harbour of New York and I remember how I wanted to go to the top. I also remember thinking how incredibly plain and geometric they were, and yet how beautiful, simple and distinguished they made the skyline of New York.

New York is one of the most exciting places in the world. Like many young South Africans, I was captivated by the city. Manhattan has an energy like no other place. You feed off it and it chases you. Everything is bigger and better in the Big Apple. At 24, I dreamed of living there – like the movie stars, business magnates and new aristocracy. After all, so many of my friends had already left the country, telling me that I would soon have to do the same. I love New York; it was my dream destination.

Many of my school buddies left South Africa. They believed that something wonderful was waiting for them overseas – in New York, London, Sydney, Toronto, Los Angeles. In some cases, they've done very well, but some ended up with working visas in low-level jobs, scrubbing floors and waiting on tables. Somehow, in a globalised world where the internet instantly connects one to everything, they were worried about geography. 'There's no future here …' or 'I couldn't raise my children here' were their protestations.

I understand how some families, particularly those touched by tragedy, would want to get away. I really wish I knew of somewhere safe to send them. The point is, and it is illustrated by the terrible events of that week, that nobody, anywhere, is safe from evil intent.

To be sentimental, Africa is in my blood. It's a tough continent: animals kill each other, people fight, and you have to work hard. Absolutely, we have problems. Crime is rampant; you take your life in your hands every time you take to our roads, walk in our cities or live on our farms. But we're good, solid people, which is why we can make it anywhere. We must clean up and sort out our own country. I'm going to try. Instead of abandoning this beautiful place, we must make it right. It is up to young South Africans to put their heads down and show some character; the fruits of our labour will be the envy of the world. In terms of what nature gives us daily, we've got a great head start.

So many people fly off to greener pastures, to places they believe will insulate them from pain, from crime or from terror. I don't want to sound cynical, but when your number's up, you go – no matter where you are. Here in South Africa, we have reason to fear, but we know that. In New York, they didn't.

White is right?

It seems like a lot of the stories in the papers are about our unhealthy obsession with race. South Africa finds itself unable to advance beyond the issue of skin colour. It's unfortunate, but it's there.

I'm happy to be white, but I don't consider it the most important thing about me. As a result, I'm not overly concerned with racial epithets and pay less attention to the idea that some other white person doing something stupid is a bad reflection on me. Other white people seem to disagree. There are some who believe in some kind of white solidarity. They must have been very sorry for it in 2001 when they read about the Waterkloof Four.

Gert van Schalkwyk, along with his mates Christoff, Frikkie and Reinach, went out one moonlit night and in cold blood *murdered* a homeless black man in a park in Pretoria. In 2005, the four were found guilty of the murder of the unidentified black man and of assaulting another. The crimes were committed when they were 16 years old and still in school. They have since repeatedly appealed their sentences, but remain guilty of murder. Taking some time off from murdering people, Christoff has made a few TV ads and Gert was at one time selected to play for the Mpumalanga Pumas (if you haven't heard of them, it's OK, they're not very good). I'm not very happy with that. Does this not make you very uncomfortable?

I took a few calls on my radio show that week and this white guy mentioned that he thought we should give them a chance. I wonder if he'd say that about a black rapist, or a corrupt black minister? I doubt it. When I asked him how he felt about crime, he said he'd be emigrating to Australia at the end of the year because of crime. Doesn't that strike you as just a little bit ironic? This guy says that crime is out of control and he is even thinking of going away forever to get away from crime, but in the same breath he thinks that I'm grossly unfair for saying that the Waterkloof Four should be in jail and that they shouldn't be given high profile jobs. I'm confused – or is he?

There are still some white people in South Africa who have come up with great new ways to disguise their contempt for blacks. How often have you observed someone complain bitterly about government, crime (always crime), service delivery and the police, and simultaneously throw away litter, gather speeding fines, park in handicapped parking bays, buy fake DVDs on the street, or perhaps do something more serious – like go into business with Glenn Agliotti?

It's the very worst kind of hypocrisy, and it stinks. If you are, as I am, sick to death of people breaking the rules, then you must accept that the rules apply equally to you. If you don't pay your taxes, or you shoot out streetlights, or you don't stop at the red lights, you're breaking the law. You're no better than the source of your ire.

I saw a guy peeing on the side of the road the other day. It all starts there. That's public indecency. The police don't need to arrest you for it to be wrong. A judge doesn't need to convict you for it to be wrong, and you don't need to be locked in jail for it to be wrong. It's just wrong. If a black man can be wrong, a white man can be just as wrong. For some people this is not a very logical thing. There are people who organise car-hijacking syndicates and run drug cartels by day and invite their affluent friends over by night. At the braai, both parties are entirely aware of the wickedness of the host's enterprises, but have the temerity to complain about government corruption while downing a beer together. It's preposterous.

Those four white guys are not going to jail for being racists; they're going to jail for murdering a man. You could be their parents, but you have to admit there is no justifiable reason for us to rally around these boys. They, just like all the other murderers in our country, are the enemy of good, law-abiding citizens and we should let them know it.

Old men and their toys

A lot of adult men need to take all their toys on holiday with them. I made this observation on my way to the seaside earlier this year, and I'm almost sorry I did …

Let me explain. On the highway at holiday time, you will see a lot of twin-cab bakkies, loaded with people and cargo, surmounted by a roof-rack with multiple bicycles attached; hitched to the back is a trailer with a Jet Ski, motorbike, canoe, speedboat and caravan. One such vehicle, whizzing by at 140km/hr, had so many things attached to it that it took two whole minutes to pass me – from front of bakkie to tip of boat engine blade.

Now I'm all for fun and games, and I suppose if you've been married to your wife for more than ten years you may need to find things to do that do not include talking to her. You need a hobby. Perhaps you hate your children because they stole your life when you were at your prime and you desire to vanquish them in a Jet Ski race, but do you really also need a caravan?

I loathe and despise caravans as much as the next guy, but my mother always said, 'Shame … Perhaps they can't afford a holiday in a house …,' and made me feel nasty for pointing and laughing. Well, that argument falls to pieces when you add up the cost of the boat, trailer, Jet Ski, bicycles, motorbike and four-wheeler, and with that cost goes my sympathy.

But I digress. We were talking about the men and their toys … Obviously these men didn't have enough toys when they were growing up, and wish to make us all suffer with them in their quest to compensate for this in later life. Here are a few hints: guys, if you're over 45 and you're bouncing around on a Jet Ski, you look like an idiot. Girls on the beach in their twenties think you're a sad old man, and your comb-over flops badly when it gets wet or windy. Your wife is embarrassed because she can hear the rude comments other people make about you while you're playing in the breakers, and she is too ashamed to bring it up when you ask her later in the day how cool you looked. You didn't look cool; you looked like the ex-pupil who hangs around your school ten years after you graduated. Lame.

Caravans, mostly popular among pikeys and gypsies, have no place on our roads. If you can afford to go on holiday at all, you can afford not to stay in a caravan. With rising fuel prices it also makes less sense to tow your motor home around, and the kinds of people you are likely to meet (and share ablution facilities with) at the trailer park are the sort of people you don't need to meet in the first place. They'll probably steal your clothes off the line and try to abduct your children, so just rent a place.

A boat is only cool if it's a yacht. Little boats are for fishermen who wear overalls, drink until their teeth fall out and smell like dockside prostitutes. If you don't have a yacht, you should rather get a surfboard and pretend you can use it. Nobody cares if your dumb boat has a cool name like *Sir Rosis of the River*, either. They'll work out pretty fast that you're not a sailor when they don't see a polished wooden deck, bright white sails and keen crew.

As for motorbikes and four-wheelers, haven't most beaches banned them? Only a total arsehole would hurtle around spraying sand on everything. Just because you shaved your head and have a tattoo doesn't mean you're hardcore. When you leave the beach people don't wish you'd come back, Koos. They wish you'd spin out of control into the rocks and have to be chiselled out in pieces by paramedics.

So in short, just go down to the beach with an umbrella, towel and, if you must, a bucket and spade. The sea is pretty exciting on its own, and I defy anyone to stand in front of those beautiful breaking waves and not find themselves contemplating their small place in the cosmos. Humility, when facing the great ocean, seems a better policy than playing around on vulgar and noisy machines.

Global warming … or is it warning?

I loathe environmental activists. They wear hemp and linen muu-muus, drive hybrid cars, eat lentils and smell like a compost heap. They have matted hair and their kids have vegetable gardens instead of toys. They yammer on about global warming and organic food. Denny Crane from *Boston Legal*, when confronted by an environmental lawyer while fishing in Canada, said: 'Don't talk to me about the environment, I'm busy enjoying nature.'

The signs are there. With the dramatic series of hurricanes, snowstorms, floods and other extreme conditions all over the world, you can't ignore changing weather patterns. I was challenged by *Elle* magazine to 'go green' for a week. How difficult could that be? I mean if Melissa Etheridge could find a rhyme for 'Inconvenient Truth' in her stupid song, I could do my bit. But it was hard. I made a checklist and started my week of giving back to the earth.

First thing I had to do was drive a Toyota Prius. Larry David from *Curb Your Enthusiasm* drives one (his ex-wife is Hollywood's biggest environmental activist, and she produced Al Gore's movie, *An Inconvenient Truth*). It's a hybrid car that uses less fuel and makes less harmful carbon emissions, or something like that. Well, this was a battle in itself. Apparently they've sold only a couple of hundred in South Africa, which means that there are more gas-guzzling Hummers on our roads than Priuses. I didn't find one. Scratch that idea.

Next thing to do was eat properly. This made sense, mostly because I had started feeling fat, and you know how I feel about fat! It wasn't easy finding the organic stuff, but once I did, I realised how much more it costs. A packet of little organic tomatoes costs about an arm and a leg more than the noxious, herbicide-coated ones, and they didn't last as long. They tasted about the same.

Perhaps I could boycott something harmful? I found a website called How To Save the World, and they have a list of products to avoid in one column and products to support on the other. There were over a hundred products to avoid (including my airline, car manufacturer, most of my favourite clothing brands, an overwhelming majority of the companies that produce all my toiletries, and virtually every food retailer in the world). In the good column were Patagonia, Abundant Earth and Green Mountain Coffee. As far as I know, Patagonia is a place, the earth is in trouble (not abundance), and I've seen a lot of coffee but none of it comes from a green mountain. So that was impossible. Scratch that.

I decided to buy some of those fluorescent, long-life light bulbs. They're brighter, environmentally friendlier and better than candles. I have also stopped using aerosols – and I intend continuing to do so. The alternatives are easy to use and can be recycled. Finally, something I could say I'd done. Replacing bulbs and using roll-on will not magically re-grow the Amazon rain forest, though …

I'd remembered to switch off lights, close the fridge door quicker, shout at a litterer, separate my rubbish and read the labels on products to see what they contained and how much harm they did – but I really didn't feel I was doing anything even remotely helpful. While you're reading this, the Japanese whalers are raping the seas; the Brazilian loggers are decimating vast swathes of virgin forest; Alaska is being mined and pillaged; and cubic kilometres of poisonous, toxic gas are being pumped into our air. How small and insignificant my petty and worthless experiment seemed. So I thought about it for a few days, and got very philosophical …

I know what the problem is. There are too many of us.

I'm not going to get depressed, though. I'm going to continue with these small green rituals, and, for what it's worth, I'm going to try to get others to do the same. A guy called my show the other day to say that the woman behind him actually got out of her car and put his cigarette butt out with her shoe. He said he couldn't believe she shouted at him. I couldn't believe he wasn't embarrassed. That woman is a bloody hero. We should all do something. Perhaps there's an environmental activist in all of us; if we can activate that, our numbers may eventually be used to nature's advantage.

Alien attack!

My parents employ a legal Malawian, whose two brothers share a small house in a township. With the horrific bouts of xenophobia this country has witnessed, I can only imagine how he must feel during these times. My parents have told him that if his brothers need to hide, they can hide with him on their property. Suddenly it's not just close to home, it's at home.

One October morning in 2008, the front page of *The Times* had a disturbing photo of a Zimbabwean man being burnt to death by a bunch of what they called 'xenophobic attackers'. The man died after receiving 100% burns all over his body. A gruesome, appalling death, one that we should all be ashamed of. It may seem like a long time ago, but the media still refer to it as the 'xenophobic outbreak of 2008'.

Some people said that this violence against mostly innocent, frightened foreign nationals started to occur because local people were unhappy about them stealing jobs, or opening township businesses. Others said the foreigners were committing crimes. I wish those people had just admitted that they were doing something that people have done for thousands of years – scapegoating. What was going on in our townships was little different to what the Nazis did to the Jews in the 1930s.

There is no statistical evidence *whatsoever* to support either the theory that foreign nationals, whether here legally or illegally, are responsible for crime or job losses. In most cases, these people should actually be classified as refugees. If I were a poor man in Zim, I'd also take my chances crawling under the border fences rather than risk the ire of Bob Mugabe. Many of these people are also industrious and desperate to make some kind of a living – a motivation some South Africans lack, sometimes because of entrenched attitudes of entitlement.

I've heard of, and seen, Somalis, Malawians, Zimbabweans and Mozambicans opening up little spaza shops and selling goods alongside the road, trying to eke out an existence. They have to live and work in constant fear of being raided by the police and threatened with deportation and extortion in return for silence – and yet they put up with it.

The latest indignity – actual physical torment and sometimes death – is simply another and more terrible burden they have to bear. The perpetrators of this violence are the very same people who hijack cars, rape old women and murder people for cellphones. How do I know? Because they're so cold and sociopathic that a simple difference in language or skin tone is enough to numb them to the cruelty of their actions. These perpetrators are the poison in our national veins. Just because someone is blacker than you, or sounds different, or has more stuff than you, you feel it's OK to burn them to death in the road. The last time this sort of thing happened it was in townships like Tembisa prior to 1994, and we don't want to go back there again, do we?

I'm glad to see all our political leaders putting aside their differences in condemning this outrageous violence. We need to detoxify our population of the people who think it acceptable to commit these terrible actions. In doing so, we may solve most of our domestic security issues simultaneously.

The meaning of life

What is life all about? It tends to happen when I go on holiday. It also happens at the beginning of a new year. I'm sure you know what I mean. You start wondering about the big scheme of things. You start pondering imponderable things, maybe because you have a little time to yourself, or maybe because those questions are the ones you're most interested in. Either way, I haven't stumbled upon some nugget of philosophical gold, and I'm no closer to working any of it out, but maybe, just maybe, you'll say: 'I was thinking about that, too!' That's good enough, then.

My friends and I started talking at a dinner about posterity and legacy. You know, what lives on after us. There were three camps. The one group said nothing lives on after us, and once we're gone nothing matters. The second group said our DNA is the only thing that matters and everything else is just that DNA trying to make more of itself. The third group said it is our ideas which give us perennial longevity.

Of course, technically, the 'nothing' group is correct, if cynical and bleak. The example that bears this out quite well is a tombstone, which is usually only ever visited by an average of two generations. It's sad, but it's true. Not much sticks around after a hundred years, let alone a thousand. We also know that in a few million years the Andromeda galaxy will start spiralling violently into our own, causing a lot of extreme temperatures, destruction and possibly our complete obliteration. Even if we survive that, our little planet will eventually be consumed either by our own sun, which will have metamorphosed into a nasty red giant, or we'll peter out into darkness and cold in the eventual heat death of the universe (where everything spreads so far away from everything else that even subatomic particles will cease to have any energy). So the real, physical future is grim.

It's likely our species will have been consigned to the rubbish dump of evolution long before any of that, unless we learn to travel in time and space, or look after our earth much better than we currently do.

The DNA group make a good case, because on a biological level we are just vehicles for DNA replication. The need to procreate and survive is programmed into all living things, because our genes want to make more of themselves. Every conscious and subconscious thing that happens is a chemical result or precursor of the purpose of that replication. The problem is that we're just puny mammals who have weaker eyes, ears, strength and speed than most other members of our class, and we tend to think we're the most advanced because our cleverness got us to where we are. We're not the fastest or the strongest and we can't fly, and if those were the criteria for determining superiority we'd lose. If you ask the drummer in a band who the most important person in a band is, he'll say the drummer. The same goes for the guitarist; he'll say guitarists. Humans like to think we're the end result of evolution, but we're imperfect and still evolving. Humans will look quite different if we live another 100 000 years. So the DNA argument is strong, but falls down thanks to random games of chance, mutations and imperfection.

So what about our ideas? Surely that is the purpose? We are, after all, sentient, conscious beings. Won't our ideas live forever? History shows they will not. Extreme cynics will say that if Newton hadn't discovered gravity, someone else would have. We know that influential thinkers (Socrates, the Prophets, Confucius) have held sway for a few thousand years, but we can't be sure that in ten thousand years anyone will remember (or care to remember) a particular author, inventor, philosopher or thinker. If our ideas give us life after death, we'd better hope that succeeding generations are careful enough to conserve them. They probably won't be.

Is there a purpose, then? What if none of these three options is correct? What if there's an architect/puppeteer/dictator/God manipulating the whole thing like a giant ant farm or Sims computer game? Would it make any difference if you knew for sure? I don't think so.

I think the real miracle isn't what happens after life; the real miracle *is* life.

Along the ancient, miserable, broken chain of evolution and cataclysmic galactic catastrophe, one small sperm cell combined in an individual and particular way with one small ovum to make you. The awe is in every moment we live and thrive. While there is life, there is something to marvel at.

If you do nothing else, *live*.

Why are we here? What's life all about?
Is God really real, or is there some doubt?
What's the point of all this hoax?
Is it the chicken and the egg time? Are we just yolks?
Or, perhaps, we're just one of God's little jokes.
Well, ça c'est le 'Meaning of Life'.
Is life just a game where we make up the rules
While we're searching for something to say,
Or are we just simply spiralling coils
Of self-replicating DNA.
In this 'life', what is our fate?
Is there Heaven and Hell? Do we reincarnate?

From Monty Python's 'Meaning of Life', by courtesy of Python (Monty) Pictures

Sweat and tears

Have you noticed that all gyms, even the clean, expensive ones, smell of sweat, chlorine and piss? I started going to gym properly about a year ago; I enjoy the exercise and the fact that I can combat ageing and corpulence by spending an hour improving my low opinion of my physical self … But I hate the gym.

First of all, there's this guy at the entrance who always shouts 'ENNNNERGY!' at me as I walk in. He can fuck off. Once inside, I have to go to the change room to get into un-sexy gym clothes. It is here that the worst offences take place. Hairy old men, naked and wrinkly, loll around the lockers and benches, displaying their saggy arses and unsightly tackle for an overly long time before dressing again. Some spread moisturiser into the cracks of their backsides, which action usually necessitates a one-leg-up-bent-over-stance I've only ever seen in bad 1970s porn. It is really very ugly. I've often wondered, looking at these old scrota, whether there are old ladies who still love them, waiting at home. I should hope not, poor women. I'm also reminded that I too will become old and undesirable one day. That scares me, properly, since I'm somewhat undesirable as it is.

Speaking of un-sexy gym clothes, this is not a true statement for some of the girls who come to my gym. A few of them tart up like they're going out for the night. You know: make-up, bare midriff, and so on. Some girls look better exercising than when they walk in. A few look like hookers, but I'm not complaining. I just think it's a waste to dress up in this environment.

Once the horror of the locker room is over, you can proceed to the cardio section, stocked with intimidating machines called elliptical walkers, static bicycles, treadmills and step-machines. Here, the fattest, oldest people trundle away many hours hoping to break a sweat and lose some flab. Some never do. I get very bored on these devices, and so try to listen to podcasts and recordings of American talk shows to make the time go by faster. Usually, someone I don't know will try to talk to me, despite my earphones, breathing difficulty and red-faced, blustery expression. They must make other friends; gym is not a social engagement for me.

By the time you get to the weight section, you will realise that gyms attract some very strange people. Big bodybuilding and weightlifting monsters dwell in the weight section. These people seldom have necks, are usually the colour of light mahogany, and make extraordinary noises while lifting impossibly large weights. They usually work in pairs, since the heaviness of their equipment carries with it the danger of death by crushing, and even they require a degree of help to get them up. Many have bald, shaven heads and wear vests (the kind where the nipples stick out and the rest clings like that plastic you use to seal dishes when you put them in the fridge). Their shorts are really very short, and sometimes you will inadvertently bear witness to their balls tumbling out – and that's just the women.

I had a wonderful personal trainer for a while; her name was Angela, and she made gym fun. Not only was she nice to look at, but she made me laugh and called me a little bitch when I told her I couldn't do any more lunges. For those who don't know, lunges are torturous exercises that involve you stretching your leg out far in front of you, plonking it down, squatting down so that your other knee touches the ground and then repeating the process with the opposite leg. I'm sure there's something against it in the Geneva Convention. Either way, Angela and I gave new nicknames to all the routines: the chest press became the 'bitch tit machine'; front dumbbell raises became 'Heil Hitlers'; and push-ups became 'poes-ups'. Finally, gym was cool. We also spoke about some of the other people we saw regularly: Big Head, a chap whose watery, disproportionally large head made up at least 60% of his total mass; She-Ra, a female bodybuilder with flat breasts that looked like plastic bags filled with just a little porridge; and Khulubuse, a fat white guy who spent hours on the treadmill, but who walked so slowly that he read a novel while doing it. I learnt that the human race is very diverse … and all the while I hoped I'd end up looking like Ryk Neethling. That didn't happen.

Since we don't walk, run, hunt for food and climb trees much anymore, the gym is just about the only place urbanised people get to do any exercise. Horrible as they are, they're very necessary. Unless you want your muscles to atrophy, your waist to expand and your life to become completely sedentary, you have to go to them. If feeling good about your body means you have to tolerate steroid junkies, other people's sweat and dodgy change rooms, so be it. Being fat is much worse.

40 … 45?

Does how old you are matter in the 21st century? We see our age very differently from the way our parents or grandparents did. Four generations ago, 50 years of age put you on the doorstep of death. Just a few years ago, 40 was middle age. Now people are saying 60 is the new 40. The basic premise is that the generations are coming closer together. The gaps are closing. Women in their forties and women in their twenties dress more alike, enjoy the same music and talk about mostly the same things. There are CEOs who haven't even reached their mid-twenties yet, and octogenarians who have no desire to retire. The ANC Youth League even says someone is a youth until they're 35. That gives a lot of us many more years of youth and excuses to be immature and say stupid things.

Madiba turned 93 this year. Most people in their nineties used to be dilly and physically beyond saving. Their minds were gone and their bodies held together by dust. At 90, Madiba hosted the biggest rock concert in the world. Things have changed beyond measure. Thanks to advances in medicine, healthy food, make-up, cosmetic surgery and drugs we have all confused a 16-year-old for a 28-year-old in a nightclub at some stage. Maybe certain rugby players more than the rest of us, but you know … If you had to guess the ages of most of the girls you meet on a night out, it would be harder now than ever before.

To show just how far things have come, a 70-year-old woman in India recently gave birth to twins. So what does this mean for you and me? It means we can relax. It means that the old biological clocks are ticking less devastatingly than they did for our great-grandparents – who were married by 20 and parents of four by age 30. It also means we can expect more from, and be expected to do more in, our lives. You'll work for a greater part of your time on the planet, you'll be younger for longer, and you'll be older for longer, too. If that sounds like a bad thing, think of how much more you could do in one lifetime than was ever possible before.

Or you can pull a Charlie Sheen, take all the drugs and wipe yourself out sooner. It's all up to you …

Intelligunt Desine

It takes all sorts of people to call in to the radio show, and sometimes the simplest interchange can unwittingly turn into a heated debate. The other day, a guy called in and asked me a question. It was quite a straightforward question and I gave a fairly simple answer, but it caused an unbelievable volume of controversy. Maybe I should have cut him off to save myself the ensuing trouble, but that's the 'stamp of our lowly origin' – we haven't evolved prescience.

He asked me if I believed in evolution. It's actually an absurd thing to say, not unlike asking someone if they believe the earth is round. It's not about what I believe; it's about what is. These things are matters of fact, not faith or opinion, and it follows that anyone who today claimed the earth was flat would be instantly dismissible as a fool. I happen to know, since I read more than a few prescribed religious texts, and since there are incontrovertible mountains of evidence in virtually every museum, university and sedimentary rock formation on the planet's surface, that my ancestors were simple primates and that I am of a branch of these primates that was lucky enough to develop sufficient pre-frontal lobe size and opposable thumbs and is now sentient.

In short, my ancestors were the same ancestors as those of the chimpanzees. Anyway, we differ from the chimps by only one half of a chromosome in each cell's total stock of DNA. That should be close enough to render most archaeological evidence a bonus.

That this matter of evolution is called *theory* is scientific nomenclature. The theory of gravity is well established, but it is also called 'theory'. Science waits to be disproved in the light of any future and better evidence. Religion operates the other way round.

This does not deter the faithful. The fanatics claim the literal truth of biblical texts. The moderates try to marry reason and science uncomfortably with folklore. Indeed, there are volumes of tautology and counter-argument that, without the slightest shred of evidence, seek to explain that all these new discoveries dovetail neatly into the stories their old books posit as fact. You hear arguments like: 'The seven days God took to make the earth weren't actually seven 24-hour days but rather millennia. God's creation is a lengthy process ...'; or 'The dinosaurs were left out because they would have confused the Old Testament readers ...' It is amazing the lengths to which these people will go to accommodate their myths and ascribe to them the hint of fact. Nevertheless, it is not my business to assault the religious texts; for people who believe them to be true, the onus is on them to prove their truth. It wouldn't help to try to prove Harry Potter true any more than the books of Exodus or Deuteronomy.

Charles Darwin published his groundbreaking, emancipatory magnum opus, *The Origin of Species*, just over one hundred and fifty years ago. It was the first (just pipping Alfred Russel Wallace to the post) cogent and deliberate attempt made by a modern scientist to understand our origins, the diversity of biology and its adaptation to change and environment. It was nothing short of earth-shattering, and remains the foundation document for modern biology, biogeography, evolutionary theory and even some genetic medicine. Without it, we'd still be struggling with basic heredity. Yet it is also one of the most controversial works ever written.

I just finished reading a 'Christian' special introduction to the Centennial edition of Darwin's *The Origin of Species*. It's a long-winded, grasping dissertation written by someone who is patently not a rational individual; it ends in a prayer asking God to forgive him for believing in evolution and accepting the idea of intelligent design. The latter is the term for the notion that life must have come about from some sort of 'design' – a divine plan or inspiration. The product of design does not reveal anything of the designer, and so you must prove it by standard scientific means – otherwise it is just an idea.

Let me speak plainly: intelligent design is a kind of post-rationalisation that seeks to prop up a discredited and irrelevant religious prophecy. It is not in any way, shape or form a science. Just because faith is enough for religion doesn't mean it is all that is required for reason. If keeping faith alive weren't the goal, there would be no reason to develop intelligent design – or, as I like to call it, Inteligunt Desine.

The fact is that creationists and intelligent design pundits fail to answer the basic question without straying into the quasi-religious. It simply doesn't help to place a creative mind at the beginning of the universe, no matter how good it might feel or how accomplished and satisfied it will let the less curious brain rest. Believers want their God to take responsibility for all the collapsing stars, failed solar systems and imploding galaxies that have left us in this tiny corner on the one planet in this petty solar system that can support life some of the time on some of its surface. They want their creator, who has filled this world with species since life began – 99% of which are extinct already – to get the credit. None of this would have made any sense to even the wisest bull-sacrificing primitive who thought every species in the world lived within walking distance of Noah's house, so it stands to reason that we cannot apply that person's limited view of the world to describe the incredible universe that science has revealed.

Before you say it, let me: of course, science hasn't got all the answers, but it has a really good track record. And just because science can't answer a question, it doesn't mean that religion can. I find it amusing that even devout people say that they believe in Satan more than they do in evolution, but they don't know much about either and when they go to hospital they act as if they think Darwin is more likely to be right.

Evolution is not about what you believe; it happened and continues to happen. To posit an equally outrageous hypothesis: it would seem odd if there were a God and he didn't reveal this first to his supporters and rather to prying and curious scientists. Or maybe if there is a God he prefers the scientists. Either way, intelligent design loses.

Judgment Day

Open our newspapers on any given day and you'll find a story about some crooked politician-turned-businessman, thieving municipal manager, or profiteering former cadre. *Kuyadabukisa!*

Although the merest hint of criminal skulduggery would shame me into resigning public office immediately, such is not the case among those caught with their hands in the public purse. Indeed, they seem almost as greedy for attention as they are for money. For now, the courts do a pretty good job of calling them what they are – thieves – but only after very long, expensive and often disgraceful trials.

This sort of thing starts at the top, I'm afraid. Just as a fish rots from the head, politicians are only as good as the worst of them. When Jacob Zuma, before he became President, was accused of fraud and corruption, I heard some shameful suggestions from weak-willed academics and illiterates alike: some said that Zuma should have been pardoned *a priori*, some that Parliament should have intervened in the judicial process. It appeared that, in the ANC, if you were popular you could also be a criminal and rise to high office – and all of this *before* a court had even pronounced its findings. As it turns out, we were spared the whole mess by the finding of that particular judge.

Sadly, it appears that the judiciary is the least respected branch of government, probably because it's much harder to place your pals on the bench in a courtroom than dozing on a bench in Parliament. Although we have many able and competent judges, we have a host of also-ran slackers with the most basic of legal qualifications and the right connections to ascend to the mightiest of offices. 'The law is not an ass,' said Mr Bumble in Charles Dickens' *Oliver Twist*, but it seems our politicians are trying their level best to prove the opposite.

Thankfully, many smart and influential people are insisting on the prevalence of the rule of law; some are even confronting the signs of lawlessness head-on. One day, our cities will have statues to commemorate a little-known man named Hugh Glenister for his bravery in protecting our collective rights – even if we're too idle or spoiled to see that they're being seized by the dissolution of parts of the machinery of justice. Remember he was the man who took the government to court over the disbanding of the Scorpions. Our new Chief Justice, Mogoeng Mogoeng (so good you have to say it twice) has a tough job ahead of him.

I would warn our political leaders that the courts are at the coalface of protecting our rights. Not only are those rights inalienable and enshrined in the first chapter of our hard-won Constitution, but they are not to be meddled with for political purposes. Once we start down that dark path, we are properly doomed. Appoint good judges, respect the institutions that dispense justice and allow the law to correct itself over time and with meticulous application of sound reason and good principles. We do not need to meddle with any of this to make it better, but meddling will almost certainly make it worse. To pervert some well-heeled wisdom, let's not jump the *Umshini Wam*.

Slipknot kills

Do you remember that horrible story about the kid who walked into his high school in Krugersdorp and slashed a fellow pupil to death? School killings are especially upsetting. There's something so awful about kids losing their innocence to violence. There's something equally awful, though, about politicians, social engineers and religious nuts twisting the violence to suit their needs.

The perpetrator of the murder was a matric student who seems to have had a predilection for rock music, masks, swords and the devil. Here's what happened afterwards, even though it shouldn't have.

Some people blamed the school or the education department, because of course, the education department is a 24-hour psycho ward that monitors the lunatic fringe of schoolkids on a constant basis.

A fantasy creature, last called upon by Hansie Cronje, took some of the blame: the devil. He was dragged into the debate, complete with pentagrams, black candles and black nail polish. As usual, if you do good things, the voice is Jesus. If you do bad things, the voice is Satan. Same imaginary voice, different bizarre activities.

Parents and educators alike insisted on metal detectors being installed at the entrances to all schools – because metal detectors not only beep when you try to smuggle in guns and swords, they also identify psychopaths or those with intent to kill. Trust me: if you want to kill, there are plenty of blunt instruments in the classroom. I can hear the kid now: 'I was going to slice up Sven today, but darn, they took my sword away at the entrance! Foiled again!'

Armchair psychologists and social commentators bemoaned the bad influence of society as a whole, citing the rise in graphic video games, angry lyrics in rock songs and violent TV shows as triggers for murderous behaviour. We all know that listening to Slipknot will automatically transform Miley Cyrus into Charles Manson.

Religious fundamentalists said that this is what happens when people abandon religious instruction for secular education. If they'd had more Bible classes, that kid would have come right. We all know that religion is the custodian of morality, right? The kid in question knew all about Jesus and the devil.

His parents and all his friends were 'shocked' or 'appalled', or 'shocked and appalled', that such a quiet, sensitive soul would commit such heinous acts. He did, and so they're clearly very bad judges of character. His parents probably didn't even know where he was that weekend; even good parents aren't objective character witnesses.

The reality is that none of this crap is to blame. This kid is a nutcase. He was chemically or emotionally imbalanced. It wasn't the school, his parents, the rock music, the devil or even bullying. It was his conscious or cloudy decision that led to a murder, and a lack of personal responsibility that will lead to his long incarceration. Humanity is not a perfect design. Guys like this prove that we are not terribly well evolved. There are some mistakes, some glitches in the system. Worse than any of this, during all the analysis, nobody bothered to spare a thought for the family of the kid who was killed.

Just RSVP

Have you ever invited a bunch of your friends out and received a 'Can I let you know tomorrow?' or 'I might be there'? I don't know about you, but there is nothing worse than someone who can't make decisions. Those responses indicate that the author has no idea of what their future holds and that they are not in charge of their own destiny. In short, they should only ever need to be invited once.

A mate of mine organised a party at his house a while ago. He invited about 20 people. It involved some planning and catering, and his kind provision of free drinks (which, knowing my friends, would have been at considerable expense). All that was required of the guests was to indicate that they would or wouldn't be coming, and to arrive.

One of the girls he invited *definitely* confirmed she would be there. She didn't pitch. Another one said she'd let him know – I think he's still waiting for her reply. Some arrived an hour after the appointed time, and some stayed until they had something better to go to. All of these have to be examples of the very worst manners imaginable.

Put yourself in the position of the person who arranges a party: he or she incurs great cost to provide food and drink, takes the trouble to find a date suitable to most people, and then spends a lot of their own time preparing for the party. Just say yes and arrive, or say no and don't. You'll find it works really well.

'RSVP' does not mean 'I will respond if I feel like it and maybe I'll pitch up if nothing better comes along.' Our grandparents used to pride themselves on such good manners – sending handwritten notes to and fro to thank each other. It was a mark of social grace and breeding. All year round there are parties, dinners, celebrations and braais. You'll be invited to a few, and you may also do the inviting. If I put you on my list, or I'm on yours, let's just stick to the rules. if I can't come I'll just say no, and if I want to come I'll say yes. Could I ask you to do the same?

Here's how you do it:

1. **Do I want to be there?**
2. **Do I like the other people who will be there (if I know who they are)?**
3. **Do I have any serious commitments that might ruin the plan?**
4. **Is there a possibility that I might not be able to make it at the last minute?**

If the answer to any of those questions is no, then say no. It doesn't matter how cool the invitation is, or how much you like them but your girlfriend hates them. If any of the answers to the four questions is no, just politely decline. In fact, copy and paste this line (you don't have to give me credit) to the invitation:

'Thanks so much for the invitation, but I'm afraid I will be unable to make it. So glad you thought of me. Have fun!'

You see, that's the only way to react other than to accept. 'I might come' or 'Let me get back to you' are not acceptable answers. Let me end by quoting a letter I wrote some time back to a good friend of mine when she couldn't make her mind up. (I have changed the facts so as not to embarrass her.)

> ***Hi Murgatreud,***
>
> ***To you, clearly, friendship is predicated on your own fair-weather whims and fancies. I may be old-fashioned, but I still like the idea of manners and of friends who value the friendship above some cheap thrill. Every invitation extended is more than food, drinks and conversation; it's about spending***

> *time and having fun with the people who enrich and add value to your experience.*
>
> *I hate to sound all sentimental, but when you've been friends with people for more than ten years, as most of us have, you don't turn them down when something better comes along.*
>
> *We are all busy people, and I'd hate it if you, or anyone else on this mailing list, thought that we're a bunch of punctual, rule-and-regulation obsessed Nazis. But I have seen friends come and go, and I know that when I invite someone today they're on a short and specific list. I'm willing to accept that my list may need another review.*
>
> *G*

While we're talking about this stuff, isn't it funny how there is always one person who organises all the social events and the others just tag along, never making any effort to reciprocate? It's also interesting to note that the people who pitch up and who do as they say are usually also the busiest people, with the most responsibility. The ones who don't are just slobs with no idea of where they'll be at lunch time, let alone in ten years' time.

Shame … he's still single

I broke up with the latest girlfriend a few months ago. Normally I wouldn't tell you this, because I know you don't care about my relationships, and even if you do, it's probably none of your business. The reason I bring it up is that it got me thinking, and I thought maybe you're thinking the same about your relationship: what do we really want?

I have had some really good relationships – I'm sure you have, too. Some have been better than others, obviously … My philosophy about relationships is: if you can't be happy in your own company, you'll never be happy with someone else. In other words, no relationship will fill the gap if you can't fill it yourself.

This may surprise some people, but not all couples are together because they want to be. Some people are together because they're scared to be alone, or because they don't think they'll be able to find someone else. Some are together for the children, or to please their parents. Some people are together because of the money, or because it's just a convenient legal or business arrangement. Whatever their reasons, I'd rather be single until I can find a really *good* reason. To me, none of these is a good reason; they seem to come from insecurity, society's stupid norms or squalid pragmatism.

In many ways, I'm lucky. I don't have a lot of time; I have a great family and wonderful friends, and I'm not very needy, even within a relationship. But more than any of those, I really love being on my own. I don't get lonely, and so I don't need anyone right now. A lot of people don't get that: 'He must be so lonely', 'Maybe he has commitment issues …', 'Maybe he's gay', and even 'Poor guy, can't find anyone … shame.' The fact is that I like me. I'm happy with me. Not all of us need the self-validation of having someone around us all the time. I would never tell someone who's happily involved in a relationship that I thought they needed to get out, so why do some people think they need to tell me to get in?

Here's another thing that might surprise you: for some of us, our relationships are not the most important things about us. For many guys and girls, their careers, friends, pets, hobbies, holidays, books and even food can supersede relationships in priority. That's not sad unless they're sad people – and we all know you get those in relationships as well as out.

This is the year 2011; things are changing. Relationships are changing, too. Some people have a relationship that doesn't fit into the usual boxes – a relationship with themselves, the internet, their dogs. We have to be open-minded and less Victorian about things. Our President has four wives, and a geeky friend of mine just met his dream girl on a dating website. Neither of those is pathetic; they're as good as your relationship, or the lack of one.

Afghanistan!

If there were ever a place of such squalid and dry desolation, of such bitterness, violence and despair that we would have no option but to believe it was made in anger, that place would be called Afghanistan.

The country is located in a place that should make it the crossroads of the world – and for a time it was – but no road stops there, because no-one, except those born there, by a stroke of cruel fate, will stay.

Every single thing in Afghanistan is sour and ugly. The wells are poisoned; the women covered from head to toe in dusty *burqa*s; the men in matted beards with leathery, grumpy faces and the alarmingly ever-present AK-47s. The trees that grow are crooked and bear few leaves and no fruit. In winter it is arse-paralysingly cold, and in summer it is searingly hot. Rivers don't flow for much of the year and there are few wild animals to be seen. Opium is the only thing that grows and it does so at the express behest of the wickedest feudal warlords in modern history. If you can find anything redeeming about this truly horrible country, I will be happy to recant, but I don't think you will.

I read Khaled Hosseini's novel *The Kite Runner* three years ago, when people were still interested in Afghanistan. It is a lovely story, but it does no better than my description above to endear you to the place. It is an unmitigated misery.

Why am I telling you this? I tell you this because this is the country that broke one superpower in the 1980s and looks likely to break another in the 21st century. Somehow, as the opening of the movie *The Beast* (1988) will tell you, Afghanistan calls to mind the words of Rudyard Kipling from

'The Young British Soldier':

> *When you're wounded an' left on Afghanistan's plains*
> *An' the women come out to cut up your remains*
> *Jus' roll to your rifle an' blow out your brains*
> *An' go to your Gawd like a soldier*

So, will Afghanistan turn the most popular President in US history into the greatest loser? Already many Americans are agitating for the withdrawal of troops from Afghanistan. In the light of Osama bin Laden's demise, many seem to think it unnecessary for the US to remain involved in Afghanistan at all. I hope these lobbies don't win the argument. To leave now would plunge the people of Afghanistan back into the 1400s, with not a hope of catching up to modernity, civilisation or any idea of freedom. As it is, the women of Afghanistan suffer only just a little less than they did under the Taliban. Whether it has been imposed or not, the idea of elections, self-determination and a political infrastructure are starting to bear fruit in this arid place – and any kind of fruit would be welcome.

It is a great irony that any caring deity should give the very worst part of his earth to his most loyal and dedicated followers. Surely this thought must occur to Afghans – and especially to the Taliban, the former religious riot police of this severe and deeply orthodox state. You will remember them as the movement who blew up the great 6th-century human treasures once called the Buddhas of Bamiyan – pretty much the only wonders of the world Afghanistan would ever have. They were also the group that made it criminal to be a woman, and the same group that aided and abetted Osama bin Laden and his al-Qaeda lunatics.

Miles away, forgotten as soon as it is remembered, with barely anything but ash, blood and iron to chew, you may ask yourself how on earth Afghanistan might affect you?

Go to the airport. Make your way past all the checkpoints, body searches and scans, while security people rifle through your stuff to throw away half the toiletries you probably just bought. Show your passport three times more than you might once have had to, read the warnings about how jokes to do with bombs and al-Qaeda will land you in detention, and have some burly man pat down the insides of your thighs without so much as a nod of permission. That's how Afghanistan affects you.

Shower hour

Our President, he of the many wives, the charming smile, dancing and laughing, the one who is famous the world over for a rape trial, a shower, fraud allegations and dubious friends, is always in the news. Last year he had his twentieth child, with his friend Irvin Khoza's daughter. When the President forgot the name of one of his sons earlier this year, we laughed, but how on earth would you keep track?

Men with power often behave badly. Throughout history, kings, princes and chiefs have taken advantage of women who were not their wives, sometimes repeatedly. Once the big man tired of a certain wife or concubine, she would be parcelled off to a nunnery, divorced, discarded or even executed. Lately, men like Tiger Woods, Arnold Schwarzenegger, Dominique Strauss-Kahn, John Terry and John Edwards have been caught using their power for mischief with women. Even if the women consent, that doesn't make it OK, does it?

I think people's private business is their private business, but there is a duty on them to do no harm, to have a conscience and to make sure that their indiscretions (and we all have them, major or minor) don't impact badly on their responsibilities or other people. Two years ago, when Kgalema Motlanthe's private life was exposed, I stood by him. He was entitled to his privacy and he was doing his job. Would I be a hypocrite if I demanded something different from Jacob Zuma?

This has put me in a quandary. I don't believe government, religious organisations or your neighbours have any right whatsoever to interfere in your lawful, private conduct. I will stick to my guns here. I'm a social libertarian. That said, I have very serious misgivings about the present situation. My problems with the President are:

1 He's irresponsibly bringing a lot of kids into the world, and he can't be as attentive a father with so many offspring, all the more with his very busy job.

2 We have major problems in South Africa with people who can't afford to have many children having large families. It burdens the whole state with additional, unnecessary responsibilities, and adds to the environmental burden. Earth is full.

3 South Africa is at the epicentre of the HIV/AIDS pandemic. This is spread so rapidly, primarily by unprotected, multiple-partner sex. It is everyone's duty to take personal responsibility for their sexual behaviour. Putting culture and morality aside, it is a matter of life and death. The President's carelessness in this respect has already been documented.

4 He's costing the state a lot of money with his very expensive, large family. Nobody minds looking after a civil servant's justifiable expenses, but this is taking advantage.

It's a do-as-I-say situation, not do-as-I-do. It would seem that the rules are different for people in politics or people connected to politics. They are not subject to the same judgment as we ordinary people are. His comrades will excuse almost any stupid things he or his Cabinet do, because they're feathering their own nests and his presence at the top is expedient for their own ambitions. They therefore cannot be taken seriously as his moral watchdogs in this matter.

In short, Mr President, we like you but it's gotten rather muddy – both for your supporters and your detractors. Is this something you're worried about? Or is a just me? While you're thinking about that, I'm off to take a shower …

Mirror, mirror on the wall

Who is the fairest of them all? Does it even matter anymore? A few days ago, I was besieged by requests to vote for Mr South Africa. I don't think I can name one single Mr South Africa. I thought Jacob Zuma was Mr South Africa. You mean this is an actual contest? Turns out it is …

Mr South Africa is a real thing, and among some of my friends on Facebook a very important, real thing. Apparently they can win a role in *Egoli*, some fresh fruit and 17 tonnes of creatine if they win Mr South Africa, and now before my very eyes some people I actually know have materialised into contestants.

If it were just Mr South Africa, then I'd be happy to dismiss it as some sort of lunatic fringe, special-interest niche of 20 000 people looking for attention. Alas, there's Miss Body Beautiful, Mr Man-To-Watch, a host of Cleo Bachelors, Miss Tiny-Baby-Lowveld-Teen and Miss Coalfest Secunda waiting in my inbox for an endorsement. Where did all these ridiculous contests come from, and what do the people in them hope to achieve? Maybe there are nice prizes (like a lifetime supply of JC Le Roux pink sparkling wine), but why would anyone *watch* these things?

The tackiest pageants of all are the ones for little kids, where they have 5-, 6- and 7-year-olds tarted up like their coiffeured, overly made-up, plump, 1980s-throwback moms. Those events are the scariest because these poor little girls are judged by creepy grown-ups on their appearance alone. They wear grown-up clothes and do some scary dance moves and get rated out of ten by a serious-looking fashion designer, E-grade TV weather celeb or last year's winner's mom. I am sure that these contests are lodestones for paedophiles, and I cannot see why parents would want their kids to enter these things.

But let's skip right to the top: Miss South Africa. Do you know who she is? Do you even watch Miss South Africa any more?

I can't remember the last time I did. I think it was the 1980s, and the reason was that there was no other good TV on at the time. I didn't even watch Miss South Africa when a girl I was dating won it. And do you know why? Because beauty pageants are stupid. There, I said it. Someone had to say it eventually.

Beauty pageants are the most boring kind of voyeurism imaginable, for people who have no imagination and think that something good-looking is good enough if it's good-looking. It isn't, and it's very 1983. Under the apartheid government, the closest we came to seeing attractive women on TV was when Marietta Kruger read the news. She had big tits and a mole above the left one (or was it the right?). Anyway, in a kind of Afrikaner-Taliban way, sexy girls weren't allowed to appear much on TV. For some reason, the Calvinists at the SABC (or M-Net, take your pick) considered beauty pageants acceptable enough, and not too lewd, to be shown on television. These days, we can hardly change channels without some sexy girl foisting herself upon us (and a good thing it is), but it makes the beauty pageant seem quaint and outdated.

We're not grumpy, ugly people because we can't stomach beauty pageants, are we? We just need a little more. I don't want to SMS my vote for Miss South Africa or Mr Bicep Truckhoister 2009 because I don't really have an interest in the result. If you want prizes, enter the science competition at school or learn to burp 'Archbishop of Canterbury' in one breath – then I'll sponsor a decent prize for you or your kid.

Is poverty a virtue?

Poverty is an awful state of being. One would have to be monumentally callous not to have great sympathy with those who have nothing. In South Africa, a horrifying percentage of the population live in abject poverty – most unable even to feed themselves or their families. This is a terrible state of affairs – and the politicians know it.

Politicians may know there is poverty, but they seem pretty incapable of doing much about it. So they've come up with a clever plan to make us feel different about the poor – and it seems to be working. What they've done is tell us how wonderful and industrious poor people are. They (and the gullible media) fall over themselves to find stories about brave, poor people who walk many miles to work, who fetch water from wells, and who use a clever channel outside their house as a place to urinate and defecate. They tell these stories and pat the poor on the back in a gigantic, patronising gesture, and then leave them pretty much the same way they found them. We're left to feel guilty about having a flushing loo and eating sushi.

I've had enough of this guilt-tripping. I have never had sympathy with politicians, and I cannot have too much sympathy with those who fall for their cunning tricks, either. I know there are lots of people who are poor for all kinds of reasons, and we can't call all of them virtuous. Many poor people are just not very good at, or for, anything. If that statement shocks you, then the politicians' brainwashing is working on you.

Here's the deal. I pay tax. Chances are you do, too. You might even pay a lot of tax. I worked out that I work about three to five months of the year for the government. That tax money you and I pay goes to all kinds of things that are supposed to help poor people, and that's how we balance out the haves and have-nots a little. It's a bit of redistribution, and as long as we keep being successful, making a profit, the poor ought to get some help from the state. I'm sure you have no problem with any of this, unless you're a horrible person. It is calculated that you support between 10 and 60 other people through your tax money, depending on how much you earn. I don't even know who my dependants are. Do you? They might not even be terribly nice people.

My problem is that you can't have my money *and* make me feel guilty, and neither can the politicians. Otherwise, who's representing me?

I fully comprehend that some people cannot be productive – because they have no education, because they're ill, because they're tired, because they're lazy or because they have a sore right tit. But I don't want to be force-fed propaganda by left-wing socialists about how noble poor people are in their simplicity. I'm neither embarrassed to come from a good family nor embarrassed about the advantages of my birth – and if you have them, neither should you be. Some advantages are circumstantial, a result of your place and time. Just as someone with privilege cannot be filled with self-loathing over what pot luck and circumstance have given them, neither can those who have none begrudge the others for their lack of fortune. Whether you were born with a silver spoon or a wooden stick in your mouth, it's what you do with it that counts – not how you feel about it.

Debbie does Randburg

Sex on television can't be harmful unless you fall off the TV! DStv mentioned that it might consider a pay-per-view porn channel, available as a subscription service in its bouquet. Great idea. There's a market for this material, and they'd be offering a popular service to people who enjoy porn, need some help with their sex lives, or just can't get a date.

Not surprisingly, the religious community, the Department of Women, Children and the Disabled (I kid you not, there is just such a government department), Victor Matfield and a few Afrikaans singers have raised their voices in condemnation. They want, of course, to decide what you should and should not be allowed to watch in the privacy of your own home. They are the self-appointed TV police.

Let us be clear: porn is not illegal, owning porn is not illegal and viewing porn is not illegal. So, on what basis then do they claim we should oppose this offering? THE CHILDREN. This is always the last bastion of defence for any argument that has been reduced to selective and/or subjective morality. The children must be protected. As I see it, the children can't subscribe to this service anyway, so it's a moot point. The blessed children probably have free internet access courtesy of their parents, and I'm sure their cellphones are already chock-full of all kinds of filth, but the horror is reserved for a closed-market TV selection.

Their children are not DStv's problem – nor are they the problem of a government department or rugby player (I mean, what if it was Joost making the call?). Your and your children's attitude to sex and sexuality is your private business. I won't tell you how to raise them if you stop interfering with my viewing habits. For peace of mind, turn on the Crime and Investigation Network and let them watch a grisly serial murderer's up-close-and-personal life story. At least that's not blocked ...

The unhealthy and conservative approach so many South Africans have to sex and pornography is indicative of our dark and troubled past. It is also a menacing foretaste of your children's own sexually dysfunctional and prudish future. Unless we can be open-minded and start treating sex in an honest, frank way, we have no business making sweeping decisions that do nothing for morality, but do much to close minds. I'm off to buy some porn.

Pull the plug

Do you have a right to die? In Switzerland a man suffering from motor neurone disease committed assisted suicide. He switched off his own ventilator and drank a powerful poison to end his suffering. It was entirely voluntary, and his family were in attendance. He listened to Beethoven's 9th Symphony (incidentally, my favourite piece of music) and peacefully slipped away.

You can't do that in South Africa. In fact, you can only do it in Belgium, the Netherlands, Switzerland and the states of Oregon and Washington in the USA, among a few others. I have a problem with that. To my mind, neither the state, nor the church, nor my family, have any right to keep me alive if I am unwilling to stay. It is akin to telling someone who's not enjoying the party that they have to stay until the end.

You're brought into this world involuntarily, told that your life is your own all the way through it and then forbidden from ending it. It is simply not sensible. My opinion of suicide is not only that it is sensible, but also that it is an absolute right. That man in Switzerland did the hardest thing it is possible to do. I couldn't fight the survival instinct that well if I tried. He ought to be praised, not condemned. You and I have no jurisdiction over anyone else's life. Best we realise that now.

The very government that says they'll try really hard not to have you knifed in the street tries even harder to charge you (or your family, if assisted suicide) if you even attempt to end your life. In other words, if you mercifully agree to switch off your grandpa's machines when he's suffering, they will prosecute you and try to put you in jail. We must change the law. This arcane religious-canon law has no place in a modern, sensible society.

Earth is full. There is no better thing you can do than to remove yourself when you are no longer making a meaningful contribution. It is, without hyperbole, the noblest thing to do.

'Suffer the little children'

Do you know the names Karen Matthews or Nadya Suleman? You should. These are examples of women who should never have become mothers. When Jesus said 'Suffer the little children', I don't think he meant it literally.

Karen Matthews is the woman in Britain who staged her daughter Shannon's kidnapping. She did it for money, probably because she was jealous of the attention given to Madeleine McCann, and because she's a low, calculating fraudster of the worst kind. She lied about drugging, tying up and locking her daughter away in order to make money from sympathetic neighbours and concerned parents. She shed crocodile tears on Sky News and begged the 'kidnappers' to bring her back home, all the while holding the poor girl against her will in the house of her ex-lover, down the road. Well, they caught her, and she's going to jail. Still, it's a horrible story. Shows how depraved some people are.

Nadya Suleman is the woman who in 2010 gave birth to octuplets. Eight tightly packed kids, all delivered on the same day from her overpopulated uterus. Did you know she already has six other kids, aged between two and seven, and that all of her children are from different men? She is unmarried. She has an addiction to having children, and they call her the Octomom. She also lives with her parents and doesn't have a job. She plans to raise all 14 children on her own, which of course she can't, because she's poor and stupid. Honestly, the last time I saw a family that big, Julie Andrews was trying to hide them from the Nazis.

These two women have something in common, and so do the all-too-absent men who fathered their respective children. What they have in common is a complete lack of reproductive responsibility. Clearly unfit for many reasons to raise children, both went ahead and did it anyway.

The problem is that we sit with at least 15 potentially broken children and parents who are more interested in themselves than in the children they made. If you had more than 15 cats, you wouldn't be called virile; you'd be called a hoarder.

I think it must be the most amazing thing in anyone's world to have a child. To actually breed the child into existence by fertilisation isn't really much of an achievement in itself, but the feeling of responsibility and destiny must be all-encompassing. I'm terrified that I would be a bad parent, and that is why I'm not one yet. I have been told that a lot of the job comes naturally, that parents just instinctively know what to do, but it still scares me that a tiny, innocent life is created and then prone to so much imperfection and over- or under-supply of love, resources, learning, emotion and power. First-time parents are, by definition, inexperienced, and so their capacity to put a foot wrong is very great indeed.

In order to own a gun you need proficiency tests, a licence and a lot of shooting practice. The police even have to come over and check your safe to ensure you can store the gun according to the strict requirements of gun ownership legislation. If you want to drive a car, you must be over the age of 16, obtain a learner's licence, then a driver's licence, and then buy an actual car. If you want the job of CEO of a major multinational corporation, you need endless qualifications and/or years of experience, references, interviews, financial background and due diligence tests, and a multitude of talents. You see where I'm going with this?

In order to have a baby, you just need to have sex. Nothing else required. No forms, no applications; they don't even come to your house to check that the kid has space. Having a baby is easily a greater responsibility than owning the gun, getting the CEO job or driving the car, and yet anyone seems to have carte blanche, indeed the right, to reproduce. I know lots of people who make wonderful parents, but I also know lots of people who are parents and shouldn't be.

It makes me very sad and despondent when I think of all the little orphans we have in this country, not to mention the children whose parents couldn't be bothered even to feed or clothe them. To my mind, the very worst crime any human being can commit is a crime against a child. People who bring children into this world without thinking it through should be charged with malice aforethought and sterilised immediately, no questions asked. If you cannot afford, or are not responsible enough, to handle parenthood, then please don't lump this awesome responsibility on the state, granny or the community at large. It is unfair to all of us, but most of all it's unfair to your child.

I suggest that any person who wishes to become a parent fill in an application form, submitting documents that prove they are of sound mind and body, that they have adequate resources to look after the child for a good 15-18 years, that they undertake to put the child's interests before their own, and that they protect it from harm. We sign mortgage bonds for 20 years, so we can bind ourselves to parenthood contracts just as well. I believe we would have a better society if people took their reproductive responsibilities a little more seriously than they take their car purchases.

We breed because nobody can stop us, and because it's free. We should breed because we want the next generation to be better than ours. The more stupid, poor or ignorant a person is, the more likely they are to spawn offspring in large numbers and at random. These kids grow up and do the same. We're inculcating poverty and stupidity into our genes – and it will be the death of us.

Do you really have to do that? Really?

David Beckham unclogging his nose on worldwide television, men pissing next to the N1, people farting in lifts and sick individuals sneezing and coughing on you. Is it really necessary for us to be so intimate and familiar with each other's bodily functions?

A photo of Beckham blowing a blob of snot onto a football pitch during a game got me thinking: is there too much proximity? Are we too close to each other? Have you noticed that when you're the only person in an empty public bathroom with a whole row of open stalls, the next person to come in will choose the stall right next to you?

Most shrinks, TV personalities and writers talk about how we need to get closer to each other, close the gaps, get to know each other *better*. I don't entirely agree. I think distance is actually a good thing. There are very few people I need to have *close* to me. How about you? I like my space. It's not because I'm emotionally distant, aloof or phobic; I just don't crave hugs and kisses like you might. A handshake is as far as I like to go; if it's a woman, a kiss on the cheek. I don't like hugs or having my face pressed up against your smoky hair. No matter who you are.

Even a handshake, under closer inspection, is quite a dangerous thing. Doctors and scientists have found that more bugs are transferred that way than by anything you breathe in. It might be best to adopt the Japanese way of bowing the head at a distance. Problem is, we all have to change to that at the same time or there will be a lot of awkwardness.

When it comes to eating, the problem can be highlighted in Technicolor: I love going out to dinner with friends but there is always at least one person who really should have rather stayed at home. Do you really have to stuff your face like that, chew with your mouth open and then lean over and start talking and laughing? Who wants to see the food in your mouth as you're chewing? There isn't even enough warning to take cover as half-masticated food particles splatter out and inconveniently land on my plate or, even worse, on me. People who slurp soup and chew as if their mouths are trash compactors can spoil an otherwise delightful social occasion. As for burping, farting and blowing your nose, those are things none of us need to be privy to. Not me, anyway.

Closing in on my space is one thing, and I suppose I'm old-fashioned, but good manners are important to me. 'Good manners' in French are called 'savoir vivre', or 'knowing how to live'. It boils down to common courtesy, common sense and common decency. It doesn't matter how rich or poor you are, young or old, male or female, educated or not – manners maketh a man (and a woman).

The end is nigh

In May 2011, according to an 89-year-old preacher named Harold Camping, no doubt approaching his own terminus rather too slowly, the world was due to end. The latest in a long line of prophets of doom, Camping said he thought Jesus would make a return trip to earth at precisely 6pm on 21 May 2011. This return would mark an event known as the 'rapture', an event imagined and invented by evangelical Christians in the US, in which certain faithful people would be taken up into heaven, suddenly and miraculously. If a good Christian™ was 'raptured' while piloting a plane, everyone else would be doomed. If he were driving a combine harvester, he'd disappear and it would roll right over Miss Peggy-Sue's sheep. If he were chewin' 'bacca, just the 'bacca would remain. If this sounds to you like the plot of a low-budget Mel Gibson movie or an obscure (and probably discarded) Brothers Grimm fairy tale, I assure you it is not. There are a great many very silly people who believed every word of this prediction and made preparations for their world to end.

The great disappointment of neither being raptured nor being dead on 22 May seems to have been too much for Mr Camping to deal with, and so he became very quiet and slid away, subsequently suffering a stroke. His followers, including many who thought me imprudent for mocking this very risible turn of events, have fared even less well. You would think them ashamed enough to reconsider their position, but this was not the case. Many have already started to predict the next likely date for the apocalypse, so intent are they on their own, and the world's, destruction. It is important for them, I suppose, to imagine a universal end so that the nagging suspicion of their own inevitable, individual end will be in some way negated. Perhaps the end will also answer satisfactorily all their questions about an afterlife.

I'm sure only the smallest number of Camping's followers actually disposed of their assets, said their goodbyes or quit their jobs. You can be sure, though, that every single one of them believed they would be raptured, believed that gay pride had brought on the world's end (Camping's words, not mine), and judged at least a few of their friends quite ready for hell. In this, they betray their bad faith. People seem willing to say they believe a lot, but they don't give away their things just before rapture or stop crying at funerals, despite all the happiness the afterlife promises. It's a matter of instinct, it seems; actions speak louder than words.

I will not concern you with what is true, and what some believe, but we can say for a fact that Mr Camping was wrong and that at least the most famous truth he told was false. However much more in religion is untrue I will leave for the faithful to expose, in time, themselves. It is my business to be a sceptic, so I won't postulate anything I don't have evidence for. Mr Camping would do well to do the same if he expects to be taken seriously ever again.

If you say there is a magic tree that turns wicked children into snot, then it is up to you to prove it is so. It is not anyone else's job to disprove your allegations about the magic tree. That which is asserted without evidence may be dismissed without evidence. The same is true for the rapture and any other wild fantasies cooked up in Jerusalem, Mecca or Hicksville, Nebraska. Now stop frightening the children, and get to work. You don't need saving; the world economy does.

15 minutes of fame

'Who do you want to win *Idols*?' The woman who asked was middle-aged and friendly, with very big teeth. It was the hundredth time I had been asked that question, just on that night, but she deserved the truth: 'I don't really care who wins … It's not really that important. It's a result, but the winner is not the point.' She was aghast. It was like I had just told her that the conspiracy to kill JFK was headed by Jackie. After a few, drawn-out seconds of uncomfortable silence, she turned and walked away, fairly devastated.

It was the truth. The poor winner of *Idols* is only really there as the winner for the last five minutes of the last episode of a six-month season of the show. It is both the beginning and the apex of their music career. They can't really get bigger or better than that. They'll never have so many people invested in their singing than at the moment they win. That's what makes winning *Idols* so hard. It's like winning the lottery and being told you have an hour to live.

So, if the show isn't about the winner, what is it about? I suppose it's a journey. The laughs, the emotion, the songs, the judges, the mishaps and the performances. Actually the show is about you. It's all about the audience. That's why it gets such good ratings. Everyone sitting at home is a self-appointed judge at every step of the journey. You choose a favourite, become distraught when he or she is voted off the show, and then pick a new favourite. This process repeats itself until only two are left and you back one of them. Along the way you get some really good entertainment. Do you see now why the winner doesn't matter?

While we're talking *Idols*, it needs to be said that the best singer doesn't always win. In *American Idol* two seasons ago, Adam Lambert was clearly the most talented, the best performer, and the hungriest for success. He lost to the other guy. The other guy won because the audience is the most important thing about the show. They choose what happens. It isn't so much a talent show as it is a popularity contest. And that's OK. I know some people who have been so fired up by *Idols* that family feuds have broken out when a contestant is eliminated or saved. That's hysterical, but it's what really counts – we get roped in.

American Idol is the biggest show in the history of television. More people watched the last season than voted for Barack Obama and John McCain put together. The advertising space during the finale is the most expensive commercial time in the world. Coca-Cola spent more on their minute-long ad than they did on manufacturing their product that year. The show really is immense. Here in South Africa, our audience is substantially smaller, but *Idols* has raked in the highest ratings for any show on M-Net. Many of the winners have hardly been runaway successes once the show ended, but the ratings continue to rise.

I love hearing how *Idols* has become part of people's lives. It's very special to be part of something like that. I just wish people would stop asking me to audition them in airports, shops or public lavatories. And please, if you really love your kids, even though they are tone-deaf, don't make them cannon fodder for TV ratings.

Back to your roots

You are one half the product of your environment (nurture) and one half the product of your genes (nature). The first part depends on the way you were raised, the resources available, your own choices and decisions and your location. The second part you have no control over whatsoever.

When your parents made you from half of each of their genetic material (and, in turn, half of each of *their* parents' genetic material), they gave you DNA that defines and identifies you for your whole life. Unless you're a criminal or involved in a paternity suit, you're unlikely to have thought about this scientific curiosity very much, but you should. Why? Because it's the stuff you can't change: the way you look, the way you sound, your talents (or lack thereof), your genetic predisposition to run or fight, how clever or stupid you are, all the good stuff. So shouldn't you want to know what that stuff is?

Knowing who your ancestors are isn't a uniquely African idea, but most people (black and white) in Africa don't even know who their great-grandparents were. They kind of hope the ancestors will find them. They won't. You have to find them: I like to know whose DNA runs through my chromosomes, and it's a fascinating business trying to discover who those people were.

I have found pirates, princes, murderers and warriors among my ancestors. People born in India, New York, Jamaica, the Dutch East Indies and Palestine. There are rich people and very poor people. There are girls who had babies at 17 and men who fathered sons over the age of 60. It's a fascinating business. Some lines can be accurately traced to the 5th century. It's quite special to know the name of someone who lived more than 1500 years ago, and whose DNA still lives in you. While we're talking about

DNA, it's worth crediting those clever scientists who discovered it – Watson, Crick and Wilkins – because they helped us work out how heredity happens. Adenine goes with thymine, guanine goes with cytosine – all along that spiralling double helix that makes you you. Genetics will be the bedrock for the way we deal with inherited diseases once and for all.

So how much do you know about your ancestors?

Try drawing a chart. First, put your name on the left of a piece of paper. Then draw a line that splits in two. Put your father's name at the top and your mother's at the bottom. From each of them, draw another line that splits in two, citing their father and mother in turn. Do this as many times as you have information. It's called a pedigree. Since it doesn't include siblings or cousins or aunts and uncles, it's all about who made you. Along the way you'll find out all kinds of things about yourself, and realise that it's about as close as any of us come to immortality; the unbroken line of descent is your DNA chasing everlasting life.

If you don't know where you come from, how will you know where you're going to?

Star-struck

It can be a terrifying thing, meeting a famous person. You could freeze up, or you might say something very embarrassing. Sometimes the famous person disappoints you. Here are some tips to make the most out of meeting a celebrity.

1 Say as little as possible

They're not as interested in you as you are in them. Just say hello, like you would when you meet someone for the first time in a business meeting. When you meet the Queen, you're not even allowed to say anything unless she speaks to you first. When I met her all she said was 'How do you do?' and moved on, having shaken my hand with her white glove on. She didn't even stay to hear my answer.

2 Don't try to be clever or funny

I've seen too many boring people try to sound witty or clever and end up sounding like a dickhead. I saw someone meet a famous rugby player and comment on how he made a rubbish tackle in a provincial game. The rugby player in question ignored the guy and started talking to someone else. He has probably heard every stupid comment a hundred times. You're just another nobody trying to make an impression, and unless you're yourself, you won't.

3 Don't gush and scream and make everyone uncomfortable

You're not a girl at a Justin Bieber concert. The more of a scene you make by screaming and jumping up and down and behaving like a whore, the less time he's going to want to spend with you. Unless, of course, you are a girl at a Justin Bieber concert …

4 Don't be overly familiar or touchy-feely

This person isn't your friend. Behaving as if the celebrity is your friend in order to impress other people is a sure-fire way to chase the star away. Nobody wants to be used as a device, and celebs can spot attention-seekers from a mile away. I saw one of the guys from Collective Soul ask a girl to leave after she hung on him like an orang-utan for twenty minutes after their concert.

5 If you have to talk, don't talk about them the whole time

Talk about something interesting that happened today, something in the news, or something on TV. You're likely to have a good time and make their time more memorable if you talk about something you're both interested in. Tim Robbins and I once spent half an hour talking about South African accents in Los Angeles. Talking about yourself is just as bad.

6 Relax

I introduced Prince Philip to our headmaster, head boy and head girl when he and the Queen were in South Africa in 1994. After I had told him who they were, he turned to me and said, 'And who the hell are you?' Before I could answer, he replied for me: 'Oh, you're just a hanger-on, are you?' Defeated, I just nodded my head and smiled. He leaned in and whispered to me, 'Well, I know how you feel …,' and gestured to the Queen. Sometimes you have to let the famous person do what they do. They're very good at it.

7 Remember that meeting the star is a big deal for you, not for them

When I met Jack Nicholson at an NBA All-Star game at the Staples Center in Los Angeles, he had sunglasses on, barely acknowledged me, and just shook his head, saying 'no autographs and no photographs, please!' I didn't get the chance to tell him what a big fan I was. It didn't matter. I met Nicholson!

8 The nicest famous people are the biggest stars of all

Bill Clinton looks you in the eye, grabs your shoulder when he shakes your hand, and actually listens when you answer a question of his. I met him while he was President. He had lots of really important things to do rather than talk to some guy from South Africa (like bang Monica Lewinsky), but he really made me feel special. B-grade stars and people who have a lot to prove are always the most difficult to talk to.

9 Don't hang around

Getting a photo or a signature isn't as important as having an actual conversation with someone famous. If you've had a special moment with someone important, leave. Let your memory record the pictures and sounds. The only thing you want the other stuff for is to show off.

10 Be nice to the people around the star

They're the ones who make things happen. If you can connect with their manager, PA, agent or friends, you could end up seeing them again. While it's probably quite calculating on your part, most people never give the entourage any attention, and they'll remember you if you do.

Smoking can ruin your health

A few years ago, then Health Minister Nkosazana Dlamini-Zuma decided it was time to ban smoking and tobacco advertising. Along with the former came improvements, no doubt, in our lungs; along with the latter came an end to some really fantastic sponsorships and much media revenue.

I'm not a smoker. I've never even held a lit cigarette anywhere near my face. I'm not telling you this because I wear it as some kind of badge of honour, and my reasons aren't moral, health-related or even principled. I just don't like the smell of cigarettes. Both my parents smoke, as does my sister. At least half my friends smoke. I come back from nightclubs late at night, my hair and clothes reeking of ash and sour tobacco. I don't like any of that, but I don't hate smokers.

You know who hates smokers? Ex-smokers. I don't think any amount of advertising or sexy marketing will ever turn me to the dark side of the force. I'm just not interested. Having said that, I'll probably die from some nasty secondhand-smoke-inhalation-related disease.

Does the government, or any of the most vehement anti-tobacco activists, know what has happened since tobacco advertising was banned? I'll tell you. Like anything they try to ban, it goes underground. At events, clubs and parties, the tobacco companies pay hot-looking girls and guys to mingle with the crowd, offer them cigarettes for free and then sell them some once the free ones run out. They organise special 'by invitation only' concerts and house parties, to which only their databases of clients can get invitations. As someone who never wanted to smoke, getting one of these invites is the only reason I've ever been tempted to do so. The regulators will always find themselves playing catch-up to the cigarette peddlers, who now have no choice but to market their wares by ever more insidious means. Instead of a big annoying billboard or radio ad, we have to be approached personally and invasively by someone who offers us a light. Frankly, I preferred the Camel Man. At least I could see where the tobacco companies were spending their millions.

Government has started talking about banning alcohol advertising. Quite apart from the money this will draw out of sponsorship, television and radio, it will cost us jobs and joy. No more Miller Jet, no more cool ads, no more parties. The same dangerous, subversive – and much more effective – marketing devices once employed by Big Tobacco are already being tested by the liquor companies. The tactics that have kept the sales of tobacco on the up will be used to market alcohol once their advertising options become limited. How many free drinks will be offered before we see that banning advertising is unlikely to change behaviour? Wouldn't you rather see the liquor companies spend that substantial budget overtly, and in ways we can see, than in a covert and private way? I think government should back down. When the state starts to tell us what we are and aren't allowed to see advertised, then I start to worry about my freedom. The choice is and has always been ours; just because someone offers you a drag doesn't mean you have to take it.

Juliusisation

I wouldn't normally worry about people who talk about nationalisation and can't spell it, but this year has been all about the ANC Youth League's obsession with the term. They've been calling for the nationalisation of the mines, banks, land and just about anything else they imagine to be valuable. Interestingly, they didn't call for nationalisation of the military, existing parastatals or power utilities, not because they aren't already nationalised, but because seemingly they don't have much value.

Despite Pravin Gordhan stating emphatically that nationalisation was *not* government policy with regard to mines and banks, many people still think that because Julius says it, it will happen. These are the same people who said that when Madiba dies, all the blacks will take up arms and massacre the whites. Relax, people.

Nationalisation is the transfer of an asset from private control into state control (condescending is when people talk down to you). Since the state has proven, in almost every available example, to be a much poorer administrator and owner of assets than most big businesses, you would think it might be a hard sell for the Youth League, and that the onus might be on them to show how politicians and bureaucrats might extract more profit from mines or banks than the current owners of the said mines and banks. You would be wrong. The Youth League is pandering to the uneducated, unemployed masses who see banks and mines as vast treasure-troves of unequally distributed wealth. It all goes back a generation or two: many of these poor people saw their fathers and grandfathers toil for minimum wage while slavishly chopping the gold from the rock, only to watch the gold barons of the turn of the century live lives of unparalleled luxury and excess. Today, they themselves struggle to obtain loans from the great banks that seemingly own everything. When the Youth League thunders on about nationalisation, these poor dim people think some of that wealth will come their way. It won't.

The government is still the largest single landowner in South Africa. The state has a large stake in many mines and even some banks. Quite apart from all that, the state gets more than its pound of flesh from any profitable business within the Republic thanks to the taxes it collects. Which mines and banks would be taxed if the government owned them already? I think you see where I'm going with this ...

If I have a leaking tap, I call a plumber. If I have financial statements that need auditing, I call the accountant. If I want to dig up diamonds, I call a mining company. Mining isn't an easy business – well, not any more. Rising costs, increasingly expensive labour, accidents that kill people and diminishing quantities of underground raw materials are the least of a mine owner's problems. Thanks to the daily vagaries of currency exchange and commodity prices, no mine is guaranteed profit at all, no matter how much they produce. Running a mine is a lot more complex than running the welfare department. The latter is a spending mechanism that isn't concerned with how the income is derived; the former is a business concern. Government is very good at spending, and for income they just squeeze you and I. If government were in charge of mines and banks, guess what? You and I would be subsidising them.

In order to nationalise these hefty assets, government would also have to compensate their current owners, which would, in a monumental act of self-defeat, bankrupt the Treasury, at very least. Some say that it would cost over a trillion rand. We don't have that kind of money. If they decided to just seize them, they'd have to deal with bills, a lack of skills, disruption, some extremely bad international PR and possibly sanctions. It's seems like a bad idea because it is a bad idea.

Stop worrying about Julius and nationalisation. You're dancing to his tune. The Constitution doesn't allow for private assets to be seized unless in the most dramatic of circumstances, and the ruling party can't muster a two-thirds majority in Parliament to change any of that. The poor are disgruntled and need to be placated, and so it's just cheap political rhetoric. When you walk past a vicious dog, you throw it some meat and it leaves you alone. The idea of nationalisation is a putrid slab of meat Julius keeps distracting the unemployed with. Just remember that Julius doesn't have any more meat after he throws this piece to the dog. When it gets hungry again, it could turn on him …

Yes, Yes, Yes

Motivational speakers are annoying. When they perform for a crowd of downcast, disaffected office workers (in some attempt by management to stimulate productivity), they always seem to be trying harder to convince themselves of something than the audience. I saw one just this week, and he reminded me of how shallow is all their billowing rhetoric. It's Julius Malema, but without the real conviction. Their conviction is fake.

The motivational speaker I saw was trying to get everyone to 'think outside the box', to 'tap their unreleased potential' and 'raise their game'. At this point I realised he was like one of those sets they used on Hollywood Westerns – a big façade held up by glue and wood and pins. 'You can be anything you want to be!' Most of these people wouldn't do anything if they didn't need the money. As if to drive the hollow message home by force (since sense couldn't manage alone), he jumped around, became very high-pitched and used the kinds of hand gestures old Italian women use when someone in the village is caught raping a nun and drinking petrol. He gulped down two or more litres of water, spoke so fast that you couldn't tell if he was being sensible or streaming incoherent consciousness like Virginia Woolf and displayed the overt excitement of a nursery school child on the jungle gym. He stole 'Yes we can' from Obama and 'No you can't' from a book children read about strangers touching their private parts.

The stories he told were mostly of the kind that we covered in primary-school history: Moses crossing the Red Sea, Caesar crossing the Rubicon and Hannibal crossing the Alps. He told these stories knowing full well that nobody in his audience knew that the Rubicon was a tiny stream or that Hannibal wasn't that silver-haired guy from *The A-Team*. He told them, though, like he was there. They were full of impossible detail and exaggeration: 'Caesar galloped into the swirling current ...' The man was almost catatonic.

At one point he realised he had lost someone in the crowd, and snorted that he was 'talking to *you*', pointing an accusing finger at the poor, terrified girl. The only motivation I could imagine he achieved was to motivate everyone to leave at the first available opportunity. I was wrong.

At the end of his sermon, his shaven head glistening with perspiration and his shiny suit crumpled from the battle he had publicly waged against the air, he received rapturous applause. People were in awe. Many went up to thank him and take his number. Some said he had changed their lives and made them, instantly, better people. I was witnessing the foolish anoint a new prophet.

Some motivational speakers employ common sense to make an audience think they're going to benefit from his wisdom and emerge smarter and more empowered than before. For this to work, everyone has to admit that the common sense being dispensed can't be all that common. If you're blown away by the idea that you can achieve things you believe you can achieve, then you have more to worry about than being motivated. You're like a blind man bumping into walls until someone helps you remove the blindfold – only you were neither blind nor blindfolded.

Similarly, if the common sense is so common then why don't people just read it first-hand, for themselves. Everyone has access to Google, and judging by the mental acuity of most motivational speakers, gurus and consultants, they might only get it half-right. That's just common nonsense.

What do people mean when they say that something inspires them? What do they mean when they say they need motivation? I understand inspiration to be the stuff that fills you with wonder, that impresses you with truth, beauty, strength. As for motivation, that's the reason we keep trying to achieve things, right? I don't know about you, but I don't need anyone else telling me how to do that.

When you can't even motivate yourself to do something, let alone actually do it, how will a third party get it right? If, for some reason, someone telling you to tell yourself to do something you should want to do anyway is useful to you, then why choose the sort of chap who talks in circles and uses crude sales tricks that wouldn't persuade you to buy a heater in the Arctic? I just don't get it. If you need self-help, just help yourself, right?

Have you been poked?

What? You haven't been poked yet? That can mean only one thing – you aren't on Facebook. Are you one of those people who refuses to join Facebook or Twitter? You think it's bollocks because it's sedentary and rarely leads to any meaningful real-life interaction? You're missing the point. If you're not on the net, you don't exist … and you won't get poked!

Social media are more than on the ascendant. If Facebook was a country, it would be the third largest, after China and India. With Facebook's 750 million followers, and Twitter climbing with some 200 million tweeters, people are being linked up in ways we could never dream of doing in the past. I started off being sceptical. I thought it was a time-waster and a bunch of self-indulgent nonsense – people posting their photos, leaving boring status updates and adding friends they don't really have. That was until I spent some time trying to make sense of it for myself. Give it a try. If you really want to be alone, join MySpace.

As Facebook gathers momentum among older people, it's becoming something of a family reunion. Facebooking across generations can mean only one of two things – a miraculous means of bridging the age gap, or family feuds of global proportions. Your parents can now 'eavesdrop' on your conversations with friends and see those drunken party photos that previously would only be used for blackmail purposes. Family therapists have a whole new minefield of potentially explosive interchanges to navigate.

Twitter may be younger than Facebook, but it seems to be one of the fastest-growing means for breaking news and spreading gossip. It's threatening traditional news media, as eyewitnesses are tweeting events as they happen, as we saw in Egypt this year. Twitter is putting publicists' jobs at risk, as celebrities blurt out their secrets in 140 characters or less. News media don't even have to resort to phone hacking. Look at Charlie Sheen: his public firing from *Two and a Half Men* garnered him millions of Twitter followers within hours; fans (and detractors) could follow first-hand commentary from the man himself, and watch the drama unfold …

Ashton Kutcher, the so-called King of Twitter, started a trend of posting saucy personal photos … first with Demi's derrière. That was child's play. More recently, we had 'Weinergate', after Congressman Anthony Weiner posted a photo of his … wiener. At first he denied that the private parts in the photo were his, that his account had been hacked, but the Congressman soon learnt that the camera doesn't lie and on Twitter there is no place to hide. He was forced to resign, and is no doubt trying to save his family; hopefully from now on he'll take pictures in the privacy of his home.

From Chris Brown's homophobic rant to Justin Bieber fans' attack on Selena Gomez to the news that Courtney Love's tweets have finally resulted in a lawsuit, the list goes on and on. When soccer star Ryan Giggs sought an injunction to prevent newspapers from publishing allegations of an affair, 75 000 people tweeted about it. Even British Prime Minister David Cameron weighed in on the debate, saying: 'It is rather unsustainable, this situation, where newspapers can't print something that everyone else is clearly talking about.' Even Julius Malema tried to have Twitter shut down to stop his impersonators.

Social media has also changed the world of marketing and advertising. More than ever before, the way people access media is changing, with new perceptions of value and new avenues for messaging. Internationally, celebrities are already commanding huge fees to tweet sponsored messages. Social media audiences provide brands and products with new avenues to reach their consumers, in the environment where they are interacting – online.

If you haven't joined the digital revolution, it's time. You might even start to understand when your kids, friends and marketing departments talk about pokes, retweets, Twitterverse, Likes, status updates, apps, downloads, OMG, LMAO, LMFAO, ROTFLMAO, PSML, Bwaaaaahaha, along with a kind of foreign Morse code using letters instead of dots and dashes. It wud b gr8t to C U on FB. Y r u w8ting? It wud be nyc to c u on the net. Now that's where I draw the line. Call me old-fashioned. I'll take it if it means defending the English language.

Anyone for a poke? ;);)

Defending the caveman

Imagine walking through the bush and stumbling upon a 10 000-carat diamond? Well, nine-year-old Matthew Berger and his dog were treasure-hunting in the veld outside Johannesburg when they discovered something even more rare and precious.. They found a fossilised hominid – the most complete *Australopithecus sediba* skeleton ever discovered. To put this into perspective, the chances of finding such a fossil – let alone one so complete and in this condition – is like finding a needle in a haystack as big as South America. Fortunately, the boy's father happened to be Professor Lee R Berger of Wits University, who will go down in history, alongside Louis B Leakey, as one of the greatest palaeoanthropologists of all time, because of this find.

Fossils are so rare because, in order for them to be preserved at all, there need to be many environmental and circumstantial factors present from the moment of the organism's demise. Over millions of years, the conditions must also have remained fairly consistent for the fossil to remain intact, and for someone to go scratching around in just the right place requires a huge amount of luck. The fact that hominid fossils are uncommon makes the odds very small indeed. Thanks to this young man, we can now unlock a time machine to our origins and our history.

Subsequently I had the privilege of participating in the process of naming our common ancestor, *Australopithecus sediba*. Schoolkids from all over South Africa sent in suggestions for the common name for the fossil (Mrs Ples and Lucy being two other famous names for hominid skeletons). After much deliberation, we decided on the name Karabo, which means 'answer' in Setswana, and was submitted by Omphemetse Keepile, a 17-year-old student from St Mary's School in Johannesburg. That this fossil will answer many of our questions about our own past is indubitable;

the story of its discovery is, in some ways, just as remarkable.

The skeleton is of a young female hominid, and even includes a few teeth. Professor Berger thinks there may be enough material for us to one day extract just a microscopic piece of DNA, something that would represent a modern-day Rosetta Stone for the understanding of human evolution.

So why should you care about this discovery? Because if it were possible to follow your ancestral family tree back 1.78–1.95 million years ago, you'd find creatures that looked like that skeleton (obviously with all the meat and hair and features still on). That's how you would look if we wound the clock back. It wouldn't be pretty, and it would probably frighten you, but that primitive creature is an example of the narrow, miraculous chance turn that evolution took to get to you. If there were ever an appropriate use of the word 'miraculous', it would be here. I'm proud of the line of primates that led to me. I am happy to be a kind of mammal, and I think that all animals are special. I don't imagine for a minute that humans are superior to other species – or that we'll be at the top of the food chain forever. In fact, it is highly unlikely that we'll even recognise our descendants in another 100 000 years – if the earth even lasts that long.

Perhaps you also think it bizarre that so many humans consider it insulting to see our proximity to the rest of nature. People think you're being rude to them when you tell them that bonobos and chimpanzees are the closest species to our own. For many modern humans, there is a giant gulf separating us from all the other animals, as if we were almost alien to the rest of the earth's plants and animals. The truth, of course, is the happy fact that we are all made of exactly the same stuff. While we may think we're better than other creatures, we do not represent the most evolved characteristics in all fields: the osprey can see things from a mile away, while we can barely see detail over a few hundred metres. The cheetah, impala and zebra, as well as all the other primates, are faster than we are. Your domestic cat or dog can hear things on either side of the spectrum for human auditory comprehension. The two things we seem to have that have granted us such advantage – opposable thumbs and an enlarged cerebrum – would be of little use in *mano e mano* combat with a chimpanzee. While our brains and the ability to craft tools took our ancestors out of the savanna and into dominion over the whole earth, we bear the mark of creatures that still need a lot of tinkering and improvement. Our teeth, hearts and knees are built to last for a shorter time than the rest of us. We are a work in progress …

We need to be humble. Human beings are not the only great accomplishments of nature – and it will be our fault that so many great species are squeezed to the point of extinction due to our selfishness. History gives us a marvellous window through which to estimate, with perspective, the effect of immediate and daily events. So often we get caught up in our own mundane business that we forget the very improbability of our existence. This young boy's find might just help a few of us to realise it. It is one of the most precious things to have been found in our country, and if you haven't seen it, you should.

Does my bum look big in this?

I've noticed something about some people. They don't really like seeing you do well. Anything that seems to go right for you they see as something that didn't happen for them, and they begrudge you it. Some may have the decency and generosity of spirit to say 'Well done' or 'Congratulations!', but few actually mean it. It's almost like asking someone how they are – it's a politeness, but you're not in it for a long answer with a lot of detail.

As a consequence of this observation, I make a point of complimenting everyone I see do something constructive, from a small child that bubbles out the word 'Mmmmmmammma' to the intellectual who manages to break from his dreary polemics to crack a joke. I congratulate people for remembering the words to a song, for digging a nice big hole and for talking about old ladies with kindness. All of this made me realise another thing: people don't believe you when you give them a compliment any more. No doubt the two behaviour patterns are linked; because people don't compliment anyone anymore, the complimentee doesn't expect it and it washes over him or her like 'Bless you' after a sneeze – which has just become my most revolting new metaphor.

Something you may also have noticed is that there is no shortage of free advice available to you, from just about anyone regarding just about everything. There is somebody to advise you on everything from how to fly spacecraft to how to make a papier-mâché toilet. I once had a hairdresser tell me what I should buy for my brother for Christmas. In every family there's a know-it-all aunt who thinks she is an accomplished expert in everything from chemistry to child-rearing. I'm sure you also love the car guards in shopping-mall parking lots who tell you how to park and how to exit parking safely, when there can be little doubt that none of them have a licence to drive.

This advice is not given, mind you, because the people dispensing it care about you or wish you to take their advice. They do it because it makes them feel important. Again, the correct thing to do is thank them and then do the exact opposite.

Having said all this, there are a few people from whom you could accept, and believe the veracity of, a compliment. If any Members of Parliament said a nice thing about you, you'd know you were in big trouble – or that they needed money.

I once heard a woman say to her friend, quite bitchily: 'That's a great outfit! You can't even tell how fat you are.' The subject in this case took the feedback very well, in fact she seemed genuinely pleased by it. It just goes to show that even a backhanded compliment is better than no compliment at all. We should all be careful of gathering up too many compliments; they're likely to come from enemies as well as friends.

Out of this world

Why do flying saucers always seem to land in some godforsaken, rural backwater where Billy-Bob and his sister Mandy-Sue raise their eight children and grow beans? You never hear anyone in New York City claim they saw a shiny UFO skirt the Empire State Building, do you? Seriously, there are at least 20 different bits of footage from the moment of impact of the 9/11 attacks, but, since the advent of photography, not a single unidentified flying object has ever been spotted over the Big Apple. New York, bear in mind, is the home of the world's biggest news organisations. Not even the least credible of these has even a ten-second clip of, say, some little green men walking through Central Park. I think you can guess where I'm going with this ...

Could it be that the poorer, dumber and less urbanised someone is, the more likely they are to jump to conclusions about fast things in the sky that they can't identify? Most will think it's either angels or the big-eyed aliens from a Will Smith movie, but the result is always the same: the aliens land and mysteriously mutilate some cattle, torment the farmer or his family with probes, and then leave again. Sometimes they leave with the person concerned and then, more mysteriously, drop them back on earth to tell the story.

If you were one of these terrifically advanced creatures that made it here by superlative technology and a mastery of physics, wouldn't you just take what you wanted, speak to the President and avoid the simpletons in the Midwest altogether? Even if you were charmed by some farmer's daughter, I doubt you'd need to examine the fundament of a cow to obtain any knowledge your superior civilisation might have missed? Whatever you're looking for, I don't think it's up there ...

I don't know about you, but I know a few reasonably intelligent people who insist that they know what happened at Roswell in 1947, and they are sure that, based on the lack of evidence and the enormity of space, the chances are good that aliens are out there. Many brilliant scientists agree with the last part – that it is likely there are other habitable planets in the universe – but they'll want some proof before they say that it's a certainty. So far we have the not-so-credible 'eyewitness' accounts of a group of disturbed people – who seem to crave attention more than the pursuit of extraterrestrial knowledge – some grainy photographs, poor quality film footage and inconclusive radar reports. It's not exactly the Watergate Tapes.

If we were visited by aliens (and, for the sake of argument, we might have been), what would they possibly want to deal with us for? We're primitive, destructive, aggressive primates who constantly wage war against each other and the rest of the living world. We plunder our planet mercilessly and unleash dangerous nuclear weapons. If you were some stellar being passing earth invisibly, wouldn't you just give it a big skip, or would you be compelled to watch some retrogressive civilisation stumble towards extinction? I suppose we watch each other on the news, so there might be some voyeuristic pleasure to be had by these passersby. Maybe it's like a big TV show to them, or one of those simulation games where they raise the temperature every now and then to see what we'll do. I don't know if there are such creatures, but if there are, they're not going to take us very much more seriously than that.

Dear Pope

Your Holiness,

I see that you have revised the list of unpardonable and deadly sins.

We mortals must bear in mind that these are the seven sins for which death was always the prescribed punishment – hence, deadly. It has been so for two thousand years. Are you sure you want to change things? If souls last forever, there may be a few burned, stabbed, hanged, tormented sinners who will want leave to appeal from your church … Maybe more than a few. Hey, it's your church; do whatever you like.

For clarity, let me remind you and the other evildoers what the original seven deadly sins were: pride, envy, lust, sloth, greed (avarice), anger (wrath) and gluttony. That's them. The ones that would curve our spines and cause us pain and send us straight into the hottest fires of hell. It appears, Your Holiness, that you are not being quite so infallible as usual.

Forgive my cheekiness, but I have a suspicion why you decided to overturn this bit of usually unalterable dogma. Here's why you scrapped each one, and feel free to correct me if you think I'm wrong:

Pride has been transformed into the perfectly socially acceptable attribute of self-confidence. There's no need for that to be considered sinful; in fact, people with a bit of pride tend to keep their house clean.

Envy is what keeps the economy going. Your neighbour gets a cellphone that plays 'Bring Yo Booty Ova Here Bitch,' you want one, too. It's keeping up with the Joneses. It's hardly sinful, just competitive.

Lust might not be good in the eyes of your church, but the porn industry will tell you that it's almightily popular. With the divorce rate going sky-high, and with swingers, foursomes and autoerotic asphyxiation being all the rage, lust is pretty commonplace. It also keeps us breeding. Plus, what do a room full of ageing celibate virgins know about lust? And I know you don't want me to keep nagging you about priests who abuse children.

Sloth is the by-product of TV, Playstation and Nintendo Wii. The Vatican may be nice to visit, but it can't compete with Grand Theft Auto on a surround sound system, even if it makes you slothful. In any case, getting fat and pasty are punishments enough – don't make people feel bad about the one bit of excitement in their day.

Greed builds businesses. If Bill Gates wasn't greedy, he wouldn't be trying to acquire every other IT company on earth! Greed also has a positive spin; it makes us work harder to achieve extraordinary things. If Spielberg hadn't been greedy, we wouldn't have Dreamworks.

Anger is hardly OK, but is it a sin? If you're stuck in traffic in your Popemobile and your police escort takes you down the wrong processional route, don't you get angry? When they put out the wrong big, tall hat for Easter Mass, don't you get annoyed? The only people who never get angry are pot-smokers or people who have been lobotomised. Anger doesn't make you evil – it just makes you human. If you can get happy, you can get angry. Think of your mother-in-law. Oh, hang on, you don't have one.

Gluttony, the last sin, Is most difficult to avoid in 2011. McDonald's, KFC, Wimpy and Steers, with their low, low prices and saturated cooking fats, are all agents of this sin. We eat because we're unhappy, and we're unhappy because we eat. Please don't send us to hell, too!

So now we can all see why you needed to update your list of sins. If you can't make people feel bad, they'll stop asking for forgiveness – and then you'd have no power over them any more. The solution: invent new sins! What a cunning plan. I looked it up on the internet and found your new list of sins. Here they are:

- **Social inequalities and injustice**
- **Environmental pollution**
- **Morally debatable experiments**
- **Genetic manipulation**
- **Drug abuse**
- **Accumulating excessive wealth**
- **Causing poverty.**

Ta-daaaa! That's them. Let's look at them a little more closely, shall we? The first one seems well-intentioned enough, but completely impractical. One person can't really cause social injustice or inequality on the scale that, say, a church can. It's unfair to lumber the individual with that heavy responsibility. Politicians are the main culprits of this nastiness – and they're all going to Hades anyway, right?

Environmental pollution makes sense as a sin, but it's a convenient truth, and methinks the College of Cardinals know this is a great bandwagon to hop on right now. Hell, they burn environmentally unfriendly stuff just to elect you – they mustn't suddenly pretend they're close to nature.

If stem cell research – which could be the single greatest source of new cures, treatments and scientific developments for the eradication of appalling diseases – is evil (and you *do* mean stem cell research when you say 'morally debatable experiments'), then I support that sin 100% – guilty as charged. It's a sin that will bring the greatest relief to human suffering in the entire history of mankind. Jesus would have liked that a lot.

As for the fourth sin, I suppose gene splicing and 'designer babies' are what you refer to here. Your Holiness being neither a scientist nor a naturalist, I would be rude, but not incorrect, to point out that you don't know what you are talking about. Again, these technologies could eliminate cancer, Parkinson's, Alzheimer's and other horrific congenital diseases. The Vatican sees them as gifts from God.

I agree that drug abuse is terrible, but I also think people can do what they like once they're old enough to make those decisions. If people want to drink, smoke or do drugs, they should have that option – even if I don't agree with them. You wouldn't want them telling you that you *had* to do drugs, would you? It's hardly criminal to sit in your house and smoke something that calms you down after a rough day at work.

Accumulating excessive wealth is a sin! You have got to be kidding me. Pot calling the kettle black. Your Holiness, does that not make you a hypocrite? You have your own bank, own more real estate than any other incorporated institution on earth, and have gathered gold, silver and treasures from everything and everyone and everywhere. Your church is the biggest non-taxpaying business ever, one of inestimable wealth, and you must think us fools for taking you seriously on this one.

Finally, causing poverty is a bit rich (considering the previous sin). The Catholic Church actively discourages its congregants from using prophylactics like condoms and the pill. This is one of the greatest contributors to unwanted pregnancies, sexually transmitted diseases and, yes, poverty.

I think I have probably committed all of the new ones except drug abuse, and I certainly committed all of the old ones. I don't think I'm an evil person, though, and neither are most of the people I know. 'Let he who is without sin cast the first stone.'

Poor black, poor white

OK, white people, don't get all upset now. I own up to the fact that this is a generalisation, that it's provocative and that many people will disagree with everything that is about to follow. But at least admit, quietly and to yourself, that the observation is a valid one.

A casual, impartial observer will usually be able to tell you that white South Africans dress quite badly compared to their black counterparts. Having a paler skin comes with disadvantages in that certain colours look pretty awful on whites – like yellow, for example. Also, thanks in part to the bureaucrats of the old regime, whites dressed much worse under apartheid than anyone else in the world. Things like grey shoes, two-tone shirts and jeans with pleats never caught on anywhere else in the universe, but under the austere, grumpy shadow of apartheid, many ugly things took root. We're still fighting this problem, almost twenty years on.

Last week, some impoverished-looking whites pulled up next to me in their spluttering Ford Cortina on Empire Road. The driver was a man with a severely wrinkled and purple face, scrunched up like one of those things girls used to tie up their hair in the 1980s. He wore a floppy cricket hat of the kind we were forced to wear during primary school cricket matches to keep our faces from burning to a crisp in the highveld sun. It was faded, brown and very dirty. He wore a sallow, once-white-collared shirt that looked to be approaching plastic in consistency. When he got out of the car, he wasn't wearing shoes but had on a very tight pair of running shorts, pulled up very high.

His considerably less attractive mate sat in the passenger seat, scowling like someone who had discovered a human turd in her lunchbox every day since she turned five. She had very thin, patchy hair which seemed to start growing just one finger-space from the top of her eyebrows and which ended at the back in line with the tops of her ears. A cigarette bobbed precariously from her bottom lip, doing some of her talking for her. Her choice of couture for the day, from where I could see it, consisted of a billowing floral blouse, stained with food and drink of many kinds, and a pale blue jersey, pulled tight around her shoulders, in a pattern invented by someone who had no regard for regularity. When she also broke loose from the confines of the car and planted her substantial feet and tree-trunk legs on the tar, I saw that she wore sandals, brown ones.

They started to swear at each other just as the engine began to fart smoke and hiss steam. Mercifully, the lights changed just in time for me to drive away. I kept thinking about them for a while, though, and passed a black beggar. He was wearing a jacket and old but clean and polished leather shoes. The jacket had been patched up, the trousers didn't fit properly, but he looked quite respectable. He wasn't dirty or unkempt. He seemed to take some pride in his appearance, like he was aware we would see him.

For the rest of that day I forced myself to be conscious of how people dressed, and I actively looked at everyone to see if there were some general patterns for the way white and black people dressed. Disappointingly, there were. Rich people seemed, more or less, to dress well, although both the nouveau riche whites and BEE blacks were ostentatiously decked out in shiny trimmings. Whether they had any more taste than the beggar I saw earlier was debatable, but the poor people weren't as homogeneous. Poor whites were, on the whole, shabby, untidy, grimy, ragged and rough. Poor blacks wore the same things, except they wore them better, matched their colours better, and mostly kept their clothes cleaner.

Of course I have no empirical data to back this theory up, and some would argue that I know less than nothing about fashion and style, but I reckon there's some truth to it. Take a look at the pictures of whites in the 1980s and compare them to blacks then. You'll have to agree I'm at least half-right. In the meantime, I'm off to buy some Veldfokus shirts, a patch leather jacket and an elastic-waisted jean pant.

No, your baby isn't cute

It seems that being a parent – not a good or bad one, mind you, but just being a parent – imbues some people with an authority to speak about children in ways that the less fertile cannot comprehend.

A friend of mine posted a photograph of an ugly baby on Facebook the other day, commenting that not all children are beautiful. She was right; the little monster was really hideous, with a countenance that could frighten away fully grown predatory animals, with a beaming idiot smile and googly eyes like ET. She didn't identify the kid or its parents, but you would not believe the number of people she seems to have offended. There was outrage from all corners. I commented that if the baby were mine, I'd have given it up for adoption immediately. The fact that I was quite obviously joking seemed to escape many of them. Most of the comments were from people who started off by saying 'As a parent, … blah, blah, blah … disgusted.' I don't see how being a parent makes anyone more or less an aesthete. Something is either attractive or ugly, and it has nothing to do with the fulfilment of your reproductive function.

Have you noticed how some parents seem to think that they're the first human animals ever to have successfully brought a child into the world? Just because they did what all animals do naturally, and a child resulted, they anoint themselves experts in all things to do with children and even some things that have nothing to do with children. Let's be clear: there are good parents and bad ones; simply *having* the child does not mean you're in the good category. We'll only know how good you are after eighteen or more years of being a parent. So if you have a three-year-old and he's managing not to drool all over my carpets, I'm not necessarily going to dish out compliments. That would be like giving someone a 50-question examination and then telling them they'd passed after only getting to question 7. If you bear in mind that almost everybody grows up to be at least a little fucked-up, you'll see that parenthood is the kind of game where there aren't any dux scholars. It's an imperfect science in every way.

While we're talking about babies, can I ask you a favour? Don't make your baby a problem for anyone else. I won't kiss your baby, like a loathsome, toadying politician might. I'll tell you straight away that I don't like other people's children. Don't thrust it into my arms because it will cry, I'll hold it at arms length and I won't be pleased if it vomits or pees or does any of those other things a child does. Don't make me talk to it, because I don't know what to say to something small, and when I do, you and your kid will think I'm weird. (Once, watching a small boy play with toy animals I asked him which was his favourite. He said the rhinoceros. I said that was excellent, and that the Chinese would agree. He just looked at me, bewildered.) Don't ask me to babysit or change her or feed her or anything that requires that much responsibility because I will be driven to overarching terror for fear of doing something wrong.

I won't put a fence around my pool in case he toddles into my front garden and falls in. I don't want to sit and talk about the colour of his bodily functions, or watch him gurgle and splutter while I'm trying to eat lunch. You also can't just whip out a tit without asking. Just to be sure, you can't arrive with him at social engagements because you think we'll all be enamoured. Many of us will be annoyed. When you burst through the door with a hundred bags, a pram, a cot, a blanket, a playpen, toys, nappies, papooses and other equipment, I will assume you're trying to oust me from my residence, and I'll take up arms.

You had the kid, not us. Having said all this, I reserve the right to change my mind when I have my own kids.

Lead, follow or get out of the way

How often have you heard companies talk about a crisis of leadership? How often do you hear people saying that governments don't know what they're doing? If aliens landed and said 'Take me to your leader!', who would you take them to?

In the last few months, it has begun to feel like the government is paralysed. Strikes go ahead without anyone seeming able to control them; parastatals fall ever deeper into the mire; service delivery protests spread; and trade union leaders declare open war on their ANC alliance partners. There's also Julius Malema frightening the hell out of white people with his ongoing rantings, and securing more newspaper space than anyone else. Who's in charge at home?

Further afield, the messianic coming of Barack Obama in America has all but petered out into the tail end of his first term, with some respite occurring with the elimination of Osama bin Laden. That's all forgotten now, and the Republicans have gone back to opposing everything and anything Obama tries to do.

Europe freefalls into decline, and we all remain hostage to a ruthless banking system that threatens currency, trade, investment and people's savings. Whole countries, let alone banks, are bailed out, as the recession continues to tighten its grip, leaving a greater chasm between the haves and the have-nots.

The Middle East remains as unstable as ever, while revolution and instability have swept over Egypt, Tunisia, Syria, Yemen and even Gaddafi-ruled Libya.

It seems that only China, India and Brazil are in the ascendant. Who's in charge anywhere? Winston Churchill said that 'some people are born to lead, some people learn to lead and others have leadership thrust upon them', but most people here in South Africa prefer to sit around bemoaning the state of the nation and the lack of leadership.

There is a possibility that you might be the leader everyone is looking for. After all, leadership isn't a popularity contest or a job title. There is no shortage of armchair experts, but what can you *do*? Just the other day I mentioned on Facebook that I had become an ambassador for Educ8, a terrific maths and science literacy initiative. As an aside, did you know that South Africa ranks 137th out of 139 countries when it comes to maths and science literacy? Scary ...

The responses posted after my comment were, to say the least, distressing. Instead of people applauding Educ8, there were many who started trash-talking our education system, our country and our President. Believe it or not, some thick people even dragged Malema into it. We all know he's not the go-to-guy when it comes to education, unless you're teaching woodwork, right? So what do we make of this?

Imagine if everyone stood up and took responsibility for themselves and one or two other people? Problem solved! What did you do today to improve the world? Watching TV and eating chips doesn't count. If you aren't going to lead, then follow, and if you're not going to follow you better realise that you're in the way.

The king of radio

I love radio. It's the last real magic in a media world that is exponentially changing in ways that no-one could have imagined ten years ago. Radio is still about imagination, though, and ten years ago was a turning point in my life. It was then that I took over the breakfast show from John Berks on 702.

To cut a long story short, it was through a fortuitous meeting with John Berks, when I was about to be fired from Tuks FM, the campus radio station, that I was given some part-time work at 702. I was a useless producer, as John Robbie and Barry Ronge will tell you, and the only person who would have me was Kate Turkington. I love Kate, and she was the one who taught me about synchronicity. Synchronicity showed its hand when John Berks started a chain of events that made radio my career.

Unlike many broadcasters, I didn't grow up desperate to be on radio, but I did grow up listening to John Berks. I wasn't the only one. Berks (also known as Berksie, Long John Berks or LJB) stands head and shoulders above the rest as an icon of South Africa's broadcasting history. Although well known to my parents from his LM radio days, and then Swazi Music Radio, Radio 5, Capital and Springbok Radio, it was on 702 that I first heard him on the way to school in the morning. 'Did you hear what John Berks said today?' was the topic of conversation everywhere.

Berksie had an amazing array of characters: Gertjie, Poppie, Jan Sweetpak, Mrs Goldberg, Charles Fortune, Colin du Plessis, Ravi Dreamer and many others. The mornings came alive with his brilliant imitations, exercises, rail reports, his legendary fun calls, his irrepressible humour, his warmth – 'What a boykie!', his rudeness (putting callers on hold indefinitely – 'You bozo, you!') and his unpredictable competitions, which could be anything from singing families to having adults make animal noises live on the radio. With his unique sense of humour and his ability to evoke the intensity of reaction that he did, he was primarily responsible for the introduction and subsequent success of talk radio in South Africa.

When John handed the headphones over to me in 2001, he left a huge void in the lives of many listeners. He also left the Fart File. I had the honour of following in the footsteps of this living legend, and expected to inherit the secrets of success from the Master himself. What did I get? The Fart File …

Remember The Ripper? It's loud and rough, and you can't pretend it's someone else. It's a single, powerful gas explosion that comes screaming from the perpetrator. The Blower is similar to The Ripper, except it has a windy sound and always gets a laugh from bystanders. The Wet Fart is full and juicy, but be careful because it could mean bigger things are on the way. There was the common coughing fart. That's when you let out a fart and pretend it's a cough. The Slider sneaks out with an elongated wince and you hope everyone thinks it was the person next to you. Did you know that you fart about fourteen times day? Who knew? John Berks did.

John Berks is a unique human being with an extraordinary gift of being able to reach into people's hearts through their ears with his compelling voice. He had the courage and vision to forge ahead and push the boundaries in our historically divided and conservative country, where there was a paucity of choice in entertainment. He left a distinguished legacy that has enabled subsequent broadcasters and radio managers to beat the paths upon which so many have subsequently trod.

Ten years on, I had the pleasure of hosting John on my show this year. Twitter and Facebook were ablaze with comments complimenting the King of Radio and begging him to come back to the airwaves. If he did, I'd listen.

I wrote to Berks in 1998, after we'd met for the first time: 'Many people will say you were phenomenal. I was pleased to have realised this before it became retrospective.' Radio, you see, is an industry full of ego, petty jealousy and snide, suspicious, backhanded compliments. John Berks isn't like the rest; on air, he's unstoppable. Off the air, he's shy, honourable and without pretension. It seems to me that when he has a microphone in front of him, and that red light comes on, a fire starts up in his heart and he warms everyone listening. Suddenly we're all gathered around the bonfire and laughing together – and for a minute the magic of radio is completely tangible.

The morning team

Every weekday morning, a million or more people tune into 5FM to listen to great music, laugh at funny stories, get the news, catch up on what's happening, and hopefully get to work without killing someone in the traffic. You probably feel as though you know some of the people you hear every day, and you wonder what they're really like.

Who are these people you let into your bedroom every morning? I'm often asked if Damon is really as annoying as he sounds. You might want to know if Leigh-Ann really does love alcohol more than men. For the first time, I'll let you in behind-the-scenes and give you the lowdown. Thabo, Damon, Mabale, Leigh-Ann and Sias – I think of them as my second family, one more dysfunctional than the first.

There's only one person in the whole world who tells me exactly how useless I am – and she does it all the time. She's never on the air; she's not even on that list. She's a mysterious influence shrouded in wisdom and magic. Although she undoubtedly knows more about radio than all of us put together, she doesn't like attention and therefore I'll stop talking about her right now. Her name is Rina Broomberg; she is my manager, coach and friend, and when circumstances call for it she's also a witch.

I wake up at 4.30 or so. The first person I hear from is Damon, who calls me either before or just after I've woken up to check if I'm really conscious and on my way. We'll talk about Damon later, but here's how the call usually goes:

'Hello Damon. I'm awake.'

'Hello Gareth, it's Damon. Are you awake?'

'Yes, Damon.'

Then he drops the phone and I get up.

By the time I get to the studio, the producers have had a look at the news, scoured the internet and found interesting things for us to talk about. But on a good day, I don't read any of it. The day I arrive at work and struggle to find things for us to discuss, I'll know it's time to quit.

There's only one person I got to choose to work with, from the very start. We've been working together since 2001. I inherited him from John Berks as one of the most experienced engineers at 702 when I started doing the morning show there. His name is Thabo Modisane, and he's the executive producer. Here are a few things you don't know about him. Thabo is a struggle hero; he claims he was on the front page of the *Sowetan*, in the 1980s, throwing stones, although I've never seen any evidence of this. He's also happily married, and the father of two of the best-looking kids in the world – Kgosi and Masechaba – and a music graduate, saxophone player and jazz expert. Thabo has an enormous office on the 27th floor of the SABC building with a thick-pile carpet and a giant oak desk, from which he issues orders and fills his diary with expensive lunches and listening sessions. While I could manage without the others, I could never do the show without the executive producer. Some people just have a feel for what works, and Thabo's feel is spectacularly accurate, even supersensory. Thabo's only serious lack of judgment seems to have been the hiring of his assistant, Damon.

Damon is the only person like Damon on earth. I have seen characters in TV shows that come close; do you remember Paul Lassiter from *Spin City* or Larry David in *Curb Your Enthusiasm*? Damon is a real-life version of those people. He's big, strange and has no filter for tact or social grace, nor any spatial awareness. He annoys everyone, especially Leigh-Ann, and is perpetually depressed or anxious. When he isn't one of those things, he's either expelling wind from one of his orifices or eating. He is rude to callers, he takes up space, and he works from a small booth adjacent to the studio because we won't have him in the same room as us. You may think I'm being unkind – and many people who listen to us do – until you meet him. Miraculously, Damon has a lovely (if completely neurotic) wife called Bernice. He is, however, one of the most loyal and honest people I know.

Mabale used to listen to our show while studying for an honours degree in medical microbiology at UKZN. When we brought Metallica to do a concert in Durban, I asked if any blacks would like to go, and Mabale called in. Better than just a few blacks, Mabale rounded up a guy in a wheelchair, three blacks, two Indians, a Portuguese and a rough-looking lesbian couple. I gave her the tickets and asked if she wanted to come up to Johannesburg and work with us. Happily, she agreed, and even though her father never got over the disappointment, she doesn't miss petri dishes and microscopes as much as she thought she might. We like to tease Mabale because she comes from QwaQwa, and because growing up her best friend was a donkey called Motlalipule. Being young and pretty, we all assume Mabale watches *Ben 10* and Disney Channel. Mabale represents everything that is good about young people in South Africa.

When I started at 5FM, I inherited a cranky, husky sidekick from Darren Scott. I didn't like her personality and thought she was a rubbish newsreader. I asked management if we could replace her, and, as usual, they said no. After more than seven years I have still not been able to get rid of her, and her newsreading has not improved one bit. She eschews human company and drinks heavily. Her name is Leigh-Ann Mol. We call her Leigh-Ass, and just recently her family have taken to doing the same. Apart from doing the news, she's a strident animal rights activist and internet expert. Leigh-Ann is very rude to me – almost all the time – and that seems to amuse lots of people. She also farms cats, is divorced, and forgets where she parks her car. Leigh-Ann provides backing vocals on some little-known trance hits. Her bizarre form of Norwegian throat-singing is entirely unique, as is her hockey song and her very large chest area. For the record, we don't embellish Leigh-Ass's drinking problem; it's all true – only she refers to it as her drinking solution. What's not to love?

Sias gets a lot of attention for his ginger hair, and the abuse he takes for it. He's our sports coach, the father of Blake and an avid reader of the *Daily*

Sun. Sias loves all sport, and is especially good at commentating on EFC fights. Did I mention that Sias has ginger hair? He has a pretty wife, and lives about 914km away from the studio in the deep Free State, which means he has to wake up at midnight, just an hour before going to sleep. Sias is an avid Newcastle United supporter, even though he has never been to Newcastle. Like any good sportsman, Sias is a team player who plays the ball and never the man.

If I leave Jen Su out of this story, she'll be very hurt. Jen is our Hollywood reporter. Her parents were on the last sampan out of Kowloon, and made it just before Mao himself could drain the celebrity essence from young Jen. Jen has two children, has an Imelda Marcos-sized collection of hats and she takes photographs of everything. She is also likely to be seen at *every* event in South Africa, even if there are four on the same night and she walks the red carpet twice. Your event just wouldn't be A-list if you didn't invite Jen Su.

There are a few other people I should tell you about. John Schmerkowitz, Bernie Berkowitz and Arnie Malpractowitz are our resident firm of attorneys. Schmerkowitz, Berkowitz and Malpractowitz have performed services as official auditors of all our competitions, regularly represent me before the Broadcasting Complaints Commission, and have overseen complaints against Damon for dropping calls and non-performance of duties.

Do you know that in our busy, 21st-century world, some people spend more time listening to the radio than they do with their families? It's true. If you're stuck in traffic for more than an hour or two, that can sometimes be more than the quality time your wife, husband, lover or kids have with you. On a good morning, we all get along and laugh – a lot. On a bad day, the studio is like hell on wheels in a black dress. Leigh-Ann comes in hung-over, Damon annoys everyone, Thabo ignores us and Mabale takes cover. And Sias, well he has ginger bloody hair, doesn't he? If you find yourself getting irritable with me in the morning – and I hope it doesn't happen too often – just remember you're not the only one. If they're my second family, they're yours too.

Run Forrest, run!

'Don't you think those people who run the Comrades Marathon are amazing?' she said while we waited for our delayed flight to depart Bloemfontein. 'Isn't it wonderful to see their spirit, endurance and dedication?' We were watching the Durban to Maritzburg race on the TV in the boarding pen, trying to kill three wasteful hours gifted to us by 'technical problems'. 'No,' I said. 'I think running and cycling are self-indulgent and pointless for everyone except the winner.'

In any road race or cycling challenge, only one person can win. Once that person has crossed the finish line, why don't the others just give up and go home? It seems a total waste of time to carry on if you can't win. Well, to me anyway.

When I was young, we'd sit and watch those unhappy runners vomiting their way over the finish line, relieving themselves behind the bushes and forever chasing after the sinewy Bruce Fordyce. It seemed no way to spend a Sunday. There was poor, ancient Wally Hayward, hobbling the last few metres into Pietermaritzburg and looking decidedly regretful for having taken on the 89.9km in the first place. You could see he was hoping to be hit by a construction vehicle en route. This wasn't heroic; it was horrible to watch. The most dreadful part of this ordeal was the last few minutes, when some of the slowest 'runners' tried to make it before the bell sounded and counted them out. These poor, sad people try to run the clock back in their heads for a whole year, thinking that if they just took Polly Shorts with more vigour they could have won a chip of bronze. Losers. Let me save you the trouble: inevitably, the women's race is won by a formidable Russian woman with an equally formidable surname, and the men's race is over by about 10.30.

Can you tell me why marathon runners look so weak and feeble if all that running is meant to be so good for you? All of them have that bewildered, thirsty, desperate look that comes from waking up at ungodly hours to hit the streets. Many of them have tried to explain the reason they do what they do, but there isn't one. It's unreasonable to run when you can walk or drive. Usually these same people spend the week after the race complaining bitterly of stiffness in their muscles, blisters on their feet and fatigue. What did they expect?

In 490 BC, when Pheidippides ran to Sparta to warn of the impending Persian invasion, and then from Marathon to Athens to spread the news of the Greek victory, he did it because he didn't have a car. Marathons were born out of necessity, not recreation, and that is where they should have stayed. The Marathon story concludes with the unfortunate Pheidippides collapsing and dying right after his arrival. Let that be a lesson.

There is nothing special or noble about completing a running race. It's all about the runner feeling good about himself. When I want to feel good about myself, I watch Jerry Springer or masturbate. I don't expect the road to be cordoned off for that. The only good thing about runners is that they're seldom fat, and they probably won't be the prey when humans start eating each other one day. Other than that, they just buy a lot of shoes and enjoy wearing those piggy oval sunglasses.

Only the evil man runneth when nothing is chasing him.

In sickness and in health

'I hate hospitals. I hate the shiny hard floors, the metal and plastic everything, the smell of surgical spirits and industrial cleaner. I hate the queues of sickly, old, sad and tired people waiting to be put out of their misery by some uncaring, clock-watching doctor who can't wait to charge you and send you away so that they can go to their beach house with their lover – another doctor. I hate the wheelchairs, the melamine counter tops and the harsh lighting. One of the things I really despise is the host of anonymous pale prints they hang on every wall, usually of birds or shadowy figures or pots of flowers. In that respect, they have a lot in common with cheap hotels. What I mean is that I'm not a good patient, and a worse visitor to hospitals. If I'm the patient, they can drug me and keep me there, even against my will. For me to visit you in hospital, you need to be my wife, my child or my very rich, very near-death relative.

I've successfully spent my life avoiding any encounter of a medical kind, but this year I eventually yielded to having my right-hand ring finger straightened from an old sporting injury. I was happy with my crooked finger but was advised to have the surgery as a preventive measure to avoid complications in later years. The doctor said something about rheumatoid arthritis, and I pulled a face, horrified that something to do with old people was being discussed so openly in my youthful presence. The whole operation was actually less intimidating than I anticipated, and was, in fact, illuminating.

Propofol. That's the stuff they give you to make you sleep. What a marvellous concoction. It is described on the packaging as a short-acting, intravenously administered, hypnotic agent. No doubt even Julius Malema would be powerless to resist this agent. After this experience, I also began to understand why Michael Jackson hired Dr Conrad Murray as his private

Propofol-pusher. I remember them telling me that I would feel a small prick (nothing new), and decided I would try to resist the feeling as long as I could. It didn't take long. I was gone. Perfect, uninterrupted, blissful, hallucinogenic sleep. I woke up about an hour or two later, still desperate to go back to Neverland. I also woke up with a single glove on. Just like Michael Jackson! The white nurse who had sent me in to theatre was magically converted into a black nurse, who now administered attention to the pillows behind my head. The King of Pop was right; it don't matter if you're black or white, as long as you're on Propofol. Eeeeeeh-hee!

It's bad enough having to go to hospital when it's a necessity, but I find elective surgery for cosmetic purposes really baffling. With my finger still bandaged, I went off to work. I experienced no discomfort from the finger, but an inordinate amount of it from an interview I conducted with Dr Robert Rey from *Dr. 90210* on my radio show. *Dr. 90210* is a show where a bunch of Los Angeles plastic surgeons do all kinds of superficial things to make ageing, moribund and plain-looking girls more attractive. They also, on occasion, make pretty girls look ridiculous, and perfectly masculine men look like elves. So apart from being extremely irritating and self-absorbed, Dr Rey does some 15 vaginal reconstructions a day, as well as, wait for it, anal bleaching. I had heard of dying the hair to wash away the grey, and whitening the teeth, but anal bleaching? Yes. Anal bleaching. That's what Los Angeles fathers will be buying their daughters for their sweet sixteenth birthday one day. It's something porn stars started doing in the late 1990s to improve the appearance of their cloacal arrangements, and now it's all the rage. There seems to be no limit to which the self-improvement-obsessed will not go to tweak, fiddle and polish their appearance.

Here I was, reluctant to have a crooked finger fixed, and in the same hospital there are likely people booking themselves in – for the fifth time this year, no doubt – to have some lift, nip, tuck, slice, dice, chop, bleach, touch-up, correction, insertion, expansion, suction, alteration, dilution, colouration, smoothing-out, bulking-up, tidying, scarifying, tautening, shrinking or re-breaking done to their poor bodies. No wonder the medical aid companies ask you so many questions when you go into hospital. Some people will take as much elective surgery as they can get. They see their medical aid as an all-you-can-eat buffet that they need to deplete every few months. Some succeed.

But I digress. I know hospitals are places where people go to get well, and they're really good for soap opera ratings. Have you noticed how much time people spend in hospitals in the soap operas? My preference is to avoid them at all costs.

My finger is now straight. I even joked to my family that I was now perfect. They didn't laugh, and you probably won't either. My teeth, however, remain crooked. They've always been misaligned and I don't really care. My poor parents tried everything; my dentist gave me braces, which I never wore, and I'm not vain enough to go through with surgery to give me a Tom Cruise smile. I think my teeth give me character – and don't forget, vampires are very *in* at the moment.

Fantasy dinner party

Imagine you could have a dinner party. Great location, great food, great atmosphere. None of that would matter, though, because this dinner party would be unlike any other. The difference would be in the guest list. To keep it intimate, let's say that, including you, you could have any ten people – alive or dead – as company. If there's a heaven for people who, like me, love history, then this is the heaven we fantasise about.

In my dreams, I try to picture Genghis Khan devouring a leg of lamb with his hands while telling me about the invasion of Khwarezmia. I see John F Kennedy laughing when someone at the table brings up Marilyn Monroe. I can almost hear the furious religious debate between Muhammad and Bertrand Russell. I could conjure up a haughty Elizabeth I taking umbrage at Karl Marx's explanation of the power of the working classes. I allow myself to imagine every detail of Socrates' facial expression and tone while he lectures, knowing when I wake up that it's all nonsense. I don't think there is any other kind of nonsense that I wish more I could make true. Maybe this is why I love period-piece movies and historical re-enactments; they feed my brain with raw materials from which to construct detailed dreams about the characters from the past of whom I am so in awe. I hope you don't mind my self-indulgence, but while you think about your list, here is mine.

To be fair, I don't think that men and women will be equally represented around the dinner table. HIStory rather than HERstory has made this a biased exercise, and women have never been given the credit or attention they deserve by the men who chronicle the human story. I'm likely to be partial to the parts of history that fascinate me most, so the list won't be representative, or politically correct either. I also wouldn't waste too much time with those who are now alive; indeed, I'm sure you'd choose more or less the same people I might if the living were the only ones on the shortlist: Nelson Mandela, Kim Jong-Il, Barack Obama, Queen Elizabeth II, Billy Connolly, John Cleese, Angelina Jolie, Gore Vidal and Larry David, among others. I'll stick to the dead. I'll also invite them by their full honorifics, since some would never accept the invitation if it weren't in the correct form. Here, then, are my nine guests:

1 Gaius Julius Caesar Augustus, Imperator, Pater Patriae, tribunicia Potestas, Pontifex Maximus, Princeps (Emperor of Rome, 63 BC–14AD)

Founder of Western civilisation. I'd seat him to my immediate right. There are so many things we owe to Ancient Rome, but no single person presided over a more interesting stretch of human time, nor did as much to sculpt the world we now live in than the first Emperor of Rome. I cannot remember how old I was, but when I first saw a replica of the Prima Porta statue of Augustus I knew I was looking at something majestic. There is something about the pose, his expression, the kind of serenity you only ever see when someone knows who they are and exactly what they're there to do. I have been curious about Roman history ever since; it probably even predates my love of music. Augustus reformed law, imposed the Pax Romana – the longest sustained span of peace in recorded history – and seeded European culture. He gave us Virgil, and was contemporaneous with Julius Caesar, Pompey Magnus, Cicero, Cleopatra and even Jesus (though he would not have met the latter until this dinner). I'd love to hear Augustus speak of the senate, the death of Antony and Cleopatra, the ancient world and his licentious daughter Julia. Augustus would probably wear a humble linen toga and mostly look solemn. I think Churchill would make him smile. He'd be abstemious – a few olives and some bread would suffice. He once said of Rome that he 'inherited it brick and left it marble', but his last words to his wife Livia tell us just how aware he was of his place in the world. One of the few rulers to die peacefully in his bed, he turned to her and said: 'Did I play my part well? Then applaud as I exit …'

2 President Thomas Jefferson of the United States (1743–1826)

Enlightenment president-philosopher. The principal author of the Declaration of Independence would sit between Augustus and Hatshepsut. Jefferson was responsible for so much of what we refer to as our freedom in modern society. He was a champion of representative democracy, of the separation of church and state and of the condition of man. Jefferson could tell us about Washington, Franklin, Hamilton, Adams and the other founding fathers of the United States of America with wit and without reverence. He was a child of the Enlightenment in every sense of the word, and only a politician when he had to be. John Quincy Adams said of him that 'Mr. Jefferson tells large stories … you never can be an hour in this man's company without something of the marvelous, like his stories …' Jefferson apparently learned Spanish during a short, 17-day voyage, and would no doubt be able to keep everyone at the table entertained, even if Churchill and I were the only ones who could know what America was. Jefferson would be dressed like an unpretentious gentleman of the eighteenth century, probably in dull colours and with his hair tied up neatly. He probably wouldn't like hamburgers, French fries or doughnuts. In 1823, Alexander Hugh Holmes Stuart wrote, 'I have never met any one who presided at his own table, with the same playful grace and urbanity, blended with perfect dignity …' To leave Jefferson off the list would be dreadful.

3 Queen Hatshepsut, Pharaoh of Egypt (1508–1458 BC)

First woman to rule over men. Without a doubt, this woman would be entirely at ease in male company. Indeed, she had to play the role of a man throughout her life, and would have thought it right that she were placed between the most open-minded men at the table. Like Augustus, she managed to usher in an era of peace after success as a warrior early in her reign, and established trade relationships with surrounding civilisations. Hatshepsut could help us understand so much about the great kingdom of Egypt, things that archaeologists could never tell us. Though only the second-oldest guest at the table, she would also be the only one who wouldn't know a thing about any of the others, so there would be no sense of awe from her; she would probably think us all inferior and retrograde. She would also be the most magnificently dressed: resplendent in gold and jewels, with fine fabrics, and on her head the towering and bewildering united crowns of Upper and Lower Egypt – serpent and vulture – glaring at us from her forehead. Her dark, lined eyes would probably look right through you. I would, with great humility, ask her about the gods, the stone temples, the cities and palaces of the first urban settlements in Africa; I'd love to know how she kept all the men in check even though she was a woman, and I'd be fascinated to hear what an ancient Egyptian queen might think of the world we live in today. She might condescend to answer.

4 Jesus Christ of Nazareth (7–2 BC to AD 30–36)

Founder of the world's most popular religion. Whether he actually existed or not, the figure of Jesus has cast long shadows of influence and power. If he was just a man, a very special man he must have been. Being a cynic, perhaps in his presence even I might experience something of the beatific and divine, which would go some way to explaining his role in history, but to imagine him discussing truth and rights with Jefferson and Churchill might make my head explode. Jesus would probably wear some simple tunic or robe, made of wool or linen, and his trademark sandals. I don't know what he'd eat, but I'd provide fish just in case. I'd like to know what he might make of the religions of the world as they are now, of the good and bad they have done, sometimes in his name. I'd also present him with a Bible and ask him how accurately it reproduces his life and deeds. I wonder what Jesus might say to Augustus about the way Rome was governing Palestine – as an ordinary citizen today might moan to government about services or taxes. Any kind of truth, any insight into this man, might help all of humanity with some of our most pressing questions. Plus he could bring the bread and wine – and we wouldn't run out.

5 Og (Early Stone Age)

Discoverer of fire. Since our oldest guest would probably be inarticulate, we would have to have him there just to observe him. Is there a person on earth who hasn't wondered what our earliest ancestors might have looked like? Og, since he made fire, might be smarter than the rest, and we'll give him the benefit of the doubt. If it were possible for us to understand him, can you imagine how much we might learn about the slow, steady, progress of human evolution and development? Og could demonstrate, first-hand, the simplest skills and basic intelligence that likely propelled this branch of primates to eventually rule over the earth. All of this wonder and astonishment aside, I'd put him at the farthest end of the table from myself. Og would probably be naked, but if he did wear anything it would be very smelly and dirty. Jesus wouldn't judge him and Alexander would be used to battle and travel.

6 His Highness King Alexander III, King of Macedon, Hegemon of the Hellenic League, Shahanshah of Persia, Pharaoh of Egypt and Lord of Asia (356–323 BC)

Greatest warrior in history. Alexander died at age 32. I'm already older than that. By that time he had conquered the known ancient world, never lost a battle, founded cities, brought down his greatest enemies and even been declared a god in his own lifetime. The rest of us might be considered underachievers. Naturally he and Jesus (who also died in his early thirties) could squabble over their divinity while monitoring Og's behaviour. In all sincerity, I think I'd be completely star-struck by the great Alexander. All biographical detail about him suggests that he was dynamic, energetic, wild and driven like few humans before or since. Physically imposing, doubtless intelligent and certainly aware of his own power, I think he might make even Augustus quietly respectful. He'd be wearing the breastplate and armour of Macedon, with his leonine blond hair shining in the light. What really happened at the battle of Gaugamela? Were you murdered with poison? Where is your tomb? Did you love your friend Hephaestion more than you loved your wife, Roxana? Why did you let them burn Persepolis? Alexander would be able to make vivid the mythology and spectacle of a larger-than-life history. As an individual, few can have better stories to tell of Greece, Egypt, Persia, India and Bactria. I doubt any around the table would get a word in edgeways.

7 Sir Winston Leonard Spencer Churchill, Prime Minister of Great Britain (1874–1965)

Politician, man of letters, raconteur. I won't go into too detailed a biography of the man more often quoted than almost any other, but I will say that I'd be happiest to meet him. The gold standard of Britishness, the robust and bold maker of the free world and

United Nations after the Second World War, eloquent, funny, self-assured and occasionally belligerent, Churchill would no doubt consume the most liquor and have nearly the most to say. He'd wear a frock coat and tie and peer out from those soft, small eyes at the wonder of the assembly. I think, being a historian, he might derive as much joy from the occasion as I would. He would also, without doubt, stay the longest. Among kings, artists and warriors, he would set everyone at ease. Churchill's sense of humour might also make for a change from all the egotistical, political and serious philosophical conversation, and I'm sure all the guests would welcome it. I'd like to know what he thinks of the world since he departed it. I'm sure you would, too.

8 Leonardo di ser Piero da Vinci (1452–1519)

Renaissance man. There was seemingly nothing Leonardo couldn't do. He was a master painter, sculptor, architect, musician, scientist, mathematician, engineer, inventor, anatomist, geologist, cartographer, botanist and writer – and that's just the stuff we know about. When people say genius, they mean Leonardo. I doubt he would be austere and gloomy company; he'd probably be quite flashy and convivial. He'd likely wear some High Renaissance fashion and be just as interested as he would be interesting. Come to think of it, we could even get him to paint our supper. I'm more than convinced that Jefferson, across the table from him, would be his main partner in conversation, but I'm sure he'd also regale us with some unique observations about both the past and present. No man can claim to have been the master of more disciplines, skills or arts than he, and his mighty brain and creativity would ratchet the whole affair up into the rarified air of an audience with pure, undiluted talent. Giorgio Vasari said of him: 'many men and women are born with remarkable talents; but occasionally, in a way that transcends nature, a single person is marvellously endowed by Heaven with beauty, grace and talent in such abundance that he leaves other men far behind …' To omit this excellent human from our dinner party would be sinful.

9 You

Sure I could have invited some other fabled, magnificent or terrifying historical being, but I'd need someone to share this with, right? I'd need a witness and someone I could replay it with, over and over in my head. If you've read this far, you are the final guest – and you'd sit on my left and bask in the glory of some of the most phenomenal creatures ever to have graced the earth with their presence.

If there were any real genies in lamps, this dinner party would be my only wish.

Can't buy me love

Who doesn't want to be rich? The richest man in the world is a Mexican called Carlos Slim, who weighs in at a cool $75 billion. Here in South Africa we know about the Oppenheimers, Motsepes and Ruperts. South Africa has the worst Gini coefficient in the world. That doesn't mean that rubbing our lamps produces the least number of genies; it means that the gap between rich and poor is bigger than anywhere else.

Where does all the money come from, and where does it go? The last few years have seen the world held hostage by the recession, with bailouts being administered on a scale that is mind-boggling. There are zeros being added to the US deficit that they're now making up new words to describe it. The Greeks, who have been eating feta cheese and sleeping on their pretty Mediterranean islands since Socrates was just a little boy, woke up this year to a nasty surprise. Greece owes the rest of Europe a lot of money, and mighty Germany had to agree to fork out billions to save all those Greeks from being repossessed. Why am I telling you all of this?

How do you know if you're rich? As the year draws to a close, don't you wonder what you have to show for it? You work so hard, they never give you a bonus, and next year they tell you you'll have to work even harder for less money. No matter how much you earn it never seems to be enough – it's like a bottomless pit. The more we earn the more we need. Like the great philosopher Notorious B.I.G. once said, 'Mo money, mo problems!'

It's all very well being on the road to success, but life is filled with stress, anxiety, deadlines, traffic, bills, making ends meet and making relationships work. Against the background of our own financial woes is jealousy, regret, anger, revenge and, on a bigger scale, corruption. Don't you just feel powerless?

On Facebook (the real residence of wisdom) I asked: 'What are the things in life that make you rich, but that money can't buy?' Here's what people said:

Family – you love them

Values – they guide you

Choices – they shape your experiences

Friends – they are your companions through good and bad

Time – time to listen to other people when they talk, time to watch the world

Your brain – you can keep learning

Music – you can sing and dance (even if it is out of tune!)

The air, nature and the animals – but also not to own, just to witness

Laughter – all the serious people give you something to laugh at

Memories – nobody can give, buy or take those away

Your body – to enjoy everything physical. It's your vehicle

Your story – it's still unfolding, and you can write your own script

If you made a list of what you have and what you don't, which of your lists would be longer? If you ever think you're not rich, think of all the things you have that money can't buy.

If you think I'm getting all schmaltzy on you, here's an old Cliff family motto: as long as you're alive, you can always run, jump, fight, fuck, wheel a barrow or drive a truck.

So, how rich are you?

www.ingramcontent.com/pod-product-compliance
Ingram Content Group UK Ltd.
Pitfield, Milton Keynes, MK11 3LW, UK
UKHW020144250726
13967UKWH00002B/848

9 781868 424559